2022 年
中国可持续交通
发展报告

周　健　王先进　尚赞娣　编著

人民交通出版社股份有限公司

北　京

内 容 提 要

本书全面贯彻落实习近平主席在第二届联合国全球可持续交通大会开幕式上的主旨讲话精神，紧紧围绕《交通强国建设纲要》《国家综合立体交通网规划纲要》各项决策部署，按照全国交通运输工作会议具体要求，主要从基础设施、交通装备、运输服务、开放合作、安全应急、科技创新、绿色发展、交通治理等八个方面，开展了全面的分析和研究，系统总结了 2022 年我国交通运输可持续发展取得的积极成效。

本书可为各级交通运输管理部门、宏观决策部门、社会各界了解和掌握交通运输可持续发展情况提供参考。

图书在版编目（CIP）数据

2022 年中国可持续交通发展报告 / 周健，王先进，尚赞娣编著 . —北京：人民交通出版社股份有限公司，2023.12

ISBN 978-7-114-18986-9

Ⅰ. ① 2… Ⅱ. ①周… ②王… ③尚… Ⅲ. ①交通运输业—可持续性发展—研究报告—中国—2022 Ⅳ. ① F512.3

中国国家版本馆 CIP 数据核字 (2023) 第 171490 号

2022 Nian Zhongguo Kechixu Jiaotong Fazhan Baogao

书　　　名：	2022 年中国可持续交通发展报告
著 作 者：	周　健　王先进　尚赞娣
责任编辑：	吴有铭　周　宇　潘艳霞
文字编辑：	丁　遥　牛家鸣
责任校对：	孙国靖　宋佳时
责任印制：	张　凯
出版发行：	人民交通出版社股份有限公司
地　　　址：	(100011) 北京市朝阳区安定门外外馆斜街 3 号
网　　　址：	http://www.ccpcl.com.cn
销售电话：	(010) 59757973
总 经 销：	人民交通出版社股份有限公司发行部
经　　　销：	各地新华书店
印　　　刷：	北京市密东印刷有限公司
开　　　本：	889×1194　1/16
印　　　张：	10.25
字　　　数：	114 千
版　　　次：	2023 年 12 月　第 1 版
印　　　次：	2023 年 12 月　第 1 次印刷
书　　　号：	ISBN 978-7-114-18986-9
定　　　价：	80.00 元

（有印刷、装订质量问题的图书，由本公司负责调换）

编写组
DRAFTING COMMITTEE

组　长：周　健　　王先进　　尚赞娣

成　员：路敖青　　赵茜楠　　姜彩良　　李忠奎　　田春林　　萧　赓
　　　　陈徐梅　　孔亚平　　陈宗伟　　耿　红　　王望雄　　程　长
　　　　武　丽　　梁鸿旭　　徐　萍　　王雪成　　王显光　　张改平
　　　　张晚笛　　姚嘉林　　李亚敏　　陈　轩　　姚金莹　　陈嘉玉
　　　　胡许勇　　黄一帆　　桑美英　　范文涛　　黄莉莉　　陈建华
　　　　曹剑东　　胡希元　　武瑞利　　张晓征　　于丹阳　　刘柳杨
　　　　叶劲松　　王　涛　　段晓辉　　林成功　　秦芬芬　　刘　娜
　　　　王　娜　　何　涛　　张若旗　　宋晓丽　　李鹏起　　周梦婕
　　　　王　园　　张雨希　　张怡君　　张皖杉　　夏　炎　　周　雷
　　　　王锋锋　　高爱颖　　马睿君　　李　琼　　苏田田　　曹子龙
　　　　王婉佼　　罗　凯　　周艾燕　　李燕霞　　武　平　　张甜甜
　　　　郑维清　　龚露阳　　庞清阁　　闫　超　　张　晨　　刘　新
　　　　张森垚　　王明文　　赵　昕　　聂婷婷　　刘　畅　　赵　屾
　　　　刘晓菲　　刘学欣　　熊新竹　　彭建华　　江睿南　　王儒骏

前　言
PREFACE

2022 年是中国共产党和中华人民共和国历史上极为重要的一年，也是中国交通运输事业发展进程中极为重要的一年。

这一年，中国共产党第二十次全国代表大会胜利召开，擘画了全面建设社会主义现代化国家、以中国式现代化全面推进中华民族伟大复兴的宏伟蓝图。中共二十大报告强调，加快建设交通强国，对构建现代化基础设施体系、建设高效顺畅的流通体系、降低物流成本、加快推进交通运输结构调整优化、推进交通领域清洁低碳转型、强化重大基础设施安全保障体系建设、推动共建"一带一路"高质量发展等交通运输相关工作作出部署，明确了当前和今后一个时期可持续交通发展的战略方向和重点内容。

这一年，习近平主席向中国国际可持续交通创新和知识中心成立致贺信，指出"推动全球交通可持续发展、促进全球互联互通，对保障全球物流供应链稳定畅通、推动世界经济发展具有重要意义。建立中国国际可持续交通创新和知识中心是支持落实联合国 2030 年可持续发展议程的重要举措。中方愿同各国一道，充分利用中国国际可持续交通创新和知识中心平台促进全球交通合作，为推进全球发展倡议、落实联合国 2030 年可持续发展议程、推动构建人类命运共同体作出贡献"，为可持续交通发展指明了前进方向、注入了强大动力。

这一年，中国特色社会主义新时代进入第 10 个年头。中国建成了全球最大的高速铁路网、高速公路网、邮政快递网和世界级港口群，铁路、公路、水路、民航客货运输量和周转量、港口货物吞吐量、快递业务量等主要指标连续多年位居世界前列，平安交通、智慧交通、绿色交通加快推进，立体化、全方位、多层次的"一带一路"交通互联互通网络加快建设，中欧班列、远洋货轮、货运航班全力保障全球产业链供应链稳定畅通，为书写基础设施联通、贸易投资畅通、文明交融沟通的可持续发展新篇章提供了坚强保障。

这一年，中国交通运输行业完整、准确、全面贯彻新发展理念，服务加快构建新发展格局，着力推动高质量发展，全力以赴抓好交通物流保通保畅，毫不放松抓好交通运输安全生产，积极稳妥扩大交通有效投资，多措并举助企纾困，高质量综合立体交通网络加快建设，综合运输服务品质持续提升，交通运输科技创新能力进一步提高，绿色低碳交通发展稳步推进，交通运输治理水平加快提升，交通运输对外开放合作不断深化，奋力加快建设交通强国，努力当好中国式现代化的开路先锋。

这一年，中国坚持交通天下，推动落实习近平主席在第二届联合国全球可持续交通大会开幕式上提出的"坚持开放联动，推进互联互通；坚持共同发展，促进公平普惠；坚持创新驱动，增强发展动能；坚持生态优先，实现绿色低碳；坚持多边主义，完善全球治理"主张，充分发挥交通作为经济脉络和文明纽带的作用，和世界各国携手共建安全、便捷、高效、绿色、经济的现代化综合交通体系，不断加强交通运输的包容性和韧性，加快推进"人享其行、物畅其流"，交通在可持续发展的道路上稳步前行。

2023 年 9 月 25 日至 26 日，全球可持续交通高峰论坛（2023）在北京举行。为展示中国可持续交通最新进展，分享中国可持续交通发展的实践，交通运输部科学研究院编制了《2022 年中国可持续交通发展报告》，围绕基础设施、交通装备、运输服务、开放合作、安全应急、科技创新、绿色发展、交通治理等 8 个方面进行了全景式展现，以期为全球可持续交通高峰论坛（2023）提供有力的支持。

作者

2023 年 9 月

目　录
CONTENTS

一、基础设施

2022 年，中国适度超前开展交通基础设施建设，加快建设现代化高质量综合立体交通网，优化布局、结构、功能和系统集成，积极扩大交通有效投资，努力实现质的有效提升和量的合理增长。

（一）
综合立体交通网持续完善

中国持续推进综合立体交通网建设，综合交通网总里程超过 600 万公里，"6 轴 7 廊 8 通道"国家综合立体交通网主骨架空间格局基本形成，综合交通枢纽体系加快完善。

（1）铁路网广覆盖范围不断拓展。截至 2022 年末，全国铁路营业里程达到 15.5 万公里，比上年末增加 0.4 万公里。其中国家铁路营业里程 13.4 万公里，铁路路网密度 161.1 公里/万平方公里，比上年末增加 4.4 公里 / 万平方公里。铁路复线率、电化率分别为 59.6% 和 73.8%。全国高铁营业里程达 4.2 万公里，比上年末增加约 2000 公里。川藏铁路全线开工建设，亚洲最大铁路枢纽客站北京丰台站、郑渝高铁、渝厦高铁益阳至长沙段、合杭高铁湖杭段等开通运营，"八横八纵"铁路网主通道加快构建。

图 1-1　2017—2022 年铁路营业里程变化情况

图 1-2　2017—2022 年高铁营业里程变化情况

┤专栏 1-1├

北京丰台火车站正式开通运营

丰台火车站历史悠久，始建于 1895 年。2010 年，丰台站停止客运业务。2018 年实施改扩建工程。经过 4 年的改扩建，2022 年 6 月，丰台站迎来了全新面貌。

北京丰台站是国内首座采用高速、普速客运双层车场设计的特大型车站，形成"顶层高铁、地面普速、地下地铁"的立体交通模式，有效节约土地。互不干扰的站房流线体系，方便乘客换乘。这里每小时最高可容纳 14000 人同时候车，设有 32 条到达出发线，32 个客运站台面，是亚洲最大的铁路枢纽客站。

（2）公路基础设施网络化水平进一步提升。截至 2022 年末，全国公路里程 535.5 万公里，比上年末增加 7.4 万公里。公路密度 55.8 公里 / 百平方公里，比上年末增加 0.8 公里 / 百平方公里。高速公路里程 17.7 万公里，比上年末增加 0.8 万公里，其中，国家高速公路里程 12.0 万公里，比上年末增加 0.3 万公里。全国二级及以上等级公路里程 74.4 万公里，比上年末增加 2.0 万公里，占公路总里程比重为 13.9%，提高 0.2 个百分点。分行政等级看，国道里程 38.0 万公里，省道里程 39.4 万公里；农村公路里程 453.1 万公里，其中县道里程 70.0 万公里、乡道里程 124.3 万公里、村道里程 258.9 万公里。全国公路桥梁 103.3 万座、8576.5 万延米，比上年末分别增加 7.2 万座、1196.3 万延米。公路隧道 24850 处、2678.4 万延米，比上年末分别增加 1582 处、208.5 万延米。重点项目建设持续推进，G15 沈海高速公路、G55 二广高速公路两条国家高速公路网主线以及 G1523 宁波至东莞等多条国家高速公路联络线全线建成，深中通道完成多个关键工程节点，张靖皋长江大桥开工建设。

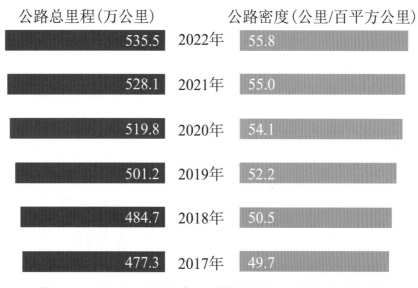

图 1-3　2017—2022 年公路总里程及公路密度变化情况

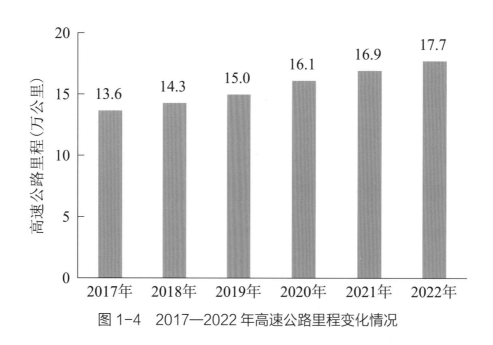

图 1-4　2017—2022 年高速公路里程变化情况

┤专栏1-2├

"四好农村路"助力乡村振兴五大工程

2022年,交通运输部门和有关部门部署启动了新一轮农村公路建设改造,重点实施"四好农村路"助力乡村振兴五大工程:

一是骨干路网提档升级工程。加快推进乡镇及主要经济节点对外快速骨干农村公路建设,有序实施老旧公路改造和过窄农村公路拓宽改造或错车道建设,强化农村公路与干线公路、城市道路以及其他运输方式的衔接。加强革命老区、民族地区、边疆地区、欠发达地区、垦区林区等农村公路建设。

二是基础路网延伸完善工程。推进农村公路建设项目更多向进村入户倾斜,因地制宜推进较大人口规模自然村(组)、抵边自然村通硬化路建设。有序实施具备条件的建制村通双车道公路建设。加强通村公路和村内道路连接,统筹规划和实施农村公路的穿村路段,兼顾村内主干道功能。

三是安全保障能力提升工程。扎实开展公路安全设施和交通秩序管理精细化提升行动,持续深化农村公路"千灯万带"示范工程,加强农村公路及其桥梁隧道隐患排查和整治,实施和完善农村公路安全生命防护工程,深入开展危旧桥梁改造。

四是产业融合发展工程。大力发展"农村公路+"模式,促进农村公路与产业深度融合发展，加快乡村产业路、旅游路、资源路建设，改善农村主要经济节点对外公路交通条件，服务乡村产业发展。

五是服务水平提升工程。以交旅融合路段为重点，完善农村公路沿线服务设施，有效利用农村客货场站、养护道班等设施，拓展开发停车、充电、购物、休闲、观光等服务功能，以信息化技术赋能农村公路高质量发展，提升农村公路服务能力和可持续发展能力。

（3）**现代化水运基础设施网络加快构建**。截至 2022 年末，全国内河航道通航里程 12.8 万公里，比上年末增加 326 公里。其中内河等级航道通航里程 6.8 万公里，占总里程比重为 52.7%，三级及以上航道通航里程 1.48 万公里，占总里程比重为 11.6%，比上年末提高 0.2 个百分点。分水系看，长江水系 64818 公里，珠江水系 16880 公里，黄河水系 3533 公里，黑龙江水系 8211 公里，京杭运河 1423 公里，闽江水系 1973 公里，淮河水系 17610 公里。西部陆海新通道平陆运河先导工程开工建设，长江中游蕲春水道航道整治工程竣工验收，江心洲至乌江河段二期等航道整治工程完工。

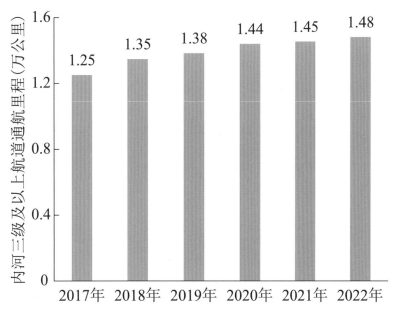

图 1-5　2017—2022 年内河三级及以上航道通航里程变化情况

┤专栏 1-3├

西部陆海新通道平陆运河工程

　　平陆运河是西部陆海新通道骨干工程，是加快建设交通强国标志性工程，始于南宁横州市西津库区平塘江口，经钦州市灵山县陆屋镇沿钦江进入北部湾，全长 134.2 公里，航道等级为内河一级，可通航 5000 吨级船舶。建设内容包括航道工程、航运枢纽工程、沿线跨河设施工程以及配套工程，其中上游至下游一次性建成马道、企石、青年 3 座双线单级 5000 吨级船闸，设计年单向通过能力 8900 万吨，预计 2026 年 12 月底主体建成。平陆运河建成后将成为中国西南地区运距最短、最经济、最便捷的出海通道。

截至 2022 年末，全国港口生产用码头泊位 21323 个，比上年末增加 456 个。沿海港口生产用码头泊位 5441 个，比上年末增加 22 个；内河港口生产用码头泊位 15882 个，比上年末增加 434 个。港口万吨级及以上泊位 2751 个，比上年末增加 92 个。其中煤炭、原油、金属矿石、集装箱等专业化万吨级及以上泊位 1468 个、比上年末增加 41 个。开工建设小洋山北侧集装箱码头工程陆域部分，建成江苏滨海液化天然气（LNG）码头工程、南通港通州湾港区吕四作业区 8~9 号泊位等重大项目。

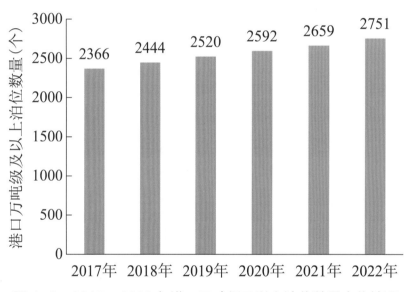

图 1-6　2017—2022 年港口万吨级及以上泊位数量变化情况

（4）民航基础设施补短板力度持续加大。截至 2022 年末，全国拥有颁证民用航空运输机场 254 个，比上年末增加 6 个，其中定期航班通航运输机场 253 个。全行业运输机场共有跑道 283 条、停机位 7315 个、航站楼面积 1798.9 万平方米，比上年末分别增加 7 条、182 个、11 万平方米。亚洲最大的专业货运机场——鄂州花湖机场建成投运，西藏山南隆子、日喀则定日机场建成通航，拉萨机场改扩建项目开工建设。全国定期航班通航城市（或地区）达到 249 个，新通航 6 个城市（或地区）分别为新疆昭苏县、阿拉尔市、塔什库尔干塔吉克自治县，湖北鄂州市，西藏山南市和日喀则市。

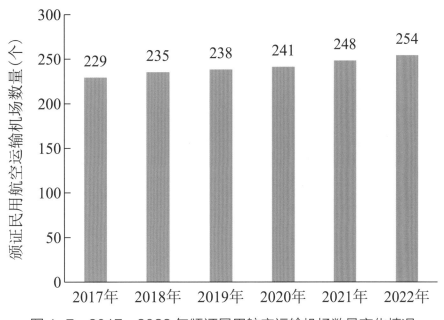

图 1-7　2017—2022 年颁证民用航空运输机场数量变化情况

（5）**邮政基础网络结构不断优化**。截至 2022 年末，全国邮政邮路总条数 4.4 万条，比上年末减少 0.2 万条，邮路总长度（单程）1142.5 万公里，比上年末减少 50.3 万公里。农村投递路线 10.4 万条，城市投递路线 11.9 万条。全行业拥有各类营业网点 43.4 万处，比上年末增加 2.1 万处，其中设在农村的 11.7 万处，比上年末增加 0.1 万处。全国拥有快递服务营业网点 23.1 万处，比上年末增加 0.3 万处❶，其中设在农村的 7.6 万处，比上年末增加 0.1 万处。快递服务网路条数 21.2 万条，比上年末增加 1.2 万条，快递服务网路长度（单程）4870.4 万公里，比上年末增加 564.8 万公里。

---

❶　四舍五入数据。

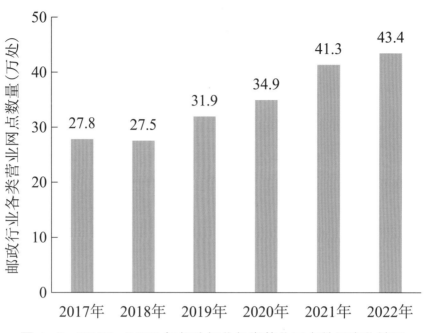

图 1-8　2017—2022 年邮政行业各类营业网点数量变化情况

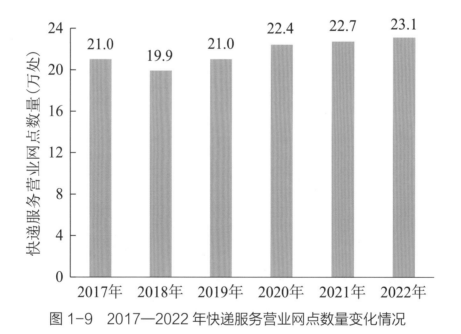

图 1-9　2017—2022 年快递服务营业网点数量变化情况

（6）城市交通设施发展稳步推进。截至 2022 年末，全国城市公交专用车道 19870 公里，比上年末增加 1607 公里。城市轨道交通运营线路 292 条，比上年末增加 17 条，运营里程总长度 9555 公里，比上年末增加 819 公里。其中地铁线路 240 条、8448 公里，轻轨线路 7 条、263 公里。全国城市公共汽电车运营线路 78020 条，比上年末增加 2250 条，运营线路总长度 166 万公里，比上年末增加 7 万公里。城市客运轮渡运营航线 79 条，比上年末减少 5 条，运营航线总长度 334.6 公里，比上年末减少 41.7 公里。

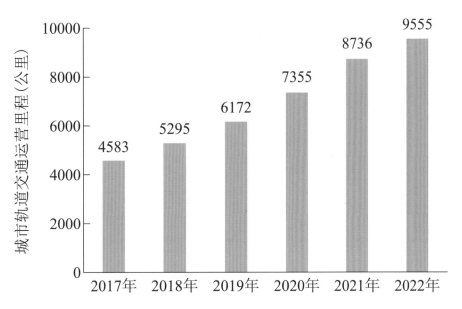

图 1-10 2017—2022 年城市轨道交通运营里程变化情况

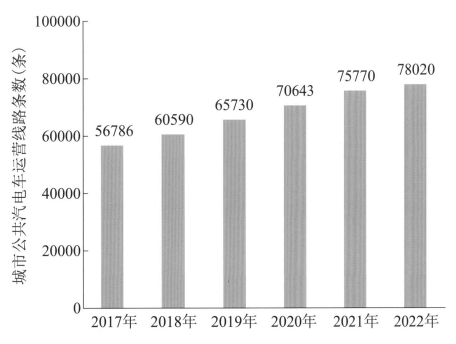

图 1-11 2017—2022 年城市公共汽电车运营线路条数变化情况

（二）
交通固定资产投资规模保持高位运行

2022 年，交通运输行业多渠道落实建设资金，加快推进重大项目建设，为稳住经济大盘作出了积极贡献。全年完成交通固定资产投资 38545 亿元，比上年增长 6.4%。其中公路、水路、民航分别完成投资 28527 亿元、1679 亿元和 1231 亿元，比上年分别增长 9.7%、10.9% 和 0.7%；铁路完成投资 7109 亿元，比上年下降 5.1%。公路建设投资中，高速公路、普通国省道投资比上年分别增长 7.3% 和 6.5%；在新一轮农村公路建设和改造带动下，农村公路投资比上年增长 15.6%。

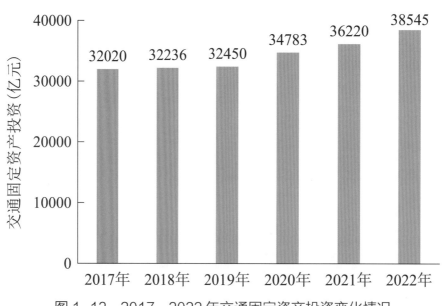

图 1-12　2017—2022 年交通固定资产投资变化情况

二、交通装备

2022 年，中国交通装备供给能力总体稳定，交通装备结构持续优化，绿色化、专业化水平持续提高。

（一）
交通装备供给能力总体稳定

（1）**铁路**。截至 2022 年末，全国拥有铁路机车 2.21 万台❶，其中内燃机车 0.78 万台，电力机车 1.42 万台，与上年末基本持平。拥有铁路客车 7.7 万辆，比上年末减少 0.02 万辆。拥有铁路货车 99.7 万辆，比上年末增加 3.1 万辆。国家统计局数据显示，2022 年全国铁路机车产量 1463 台，比上年末增长 34.8%。

（2）**公路**。截至 2022 年末，全国拥有公路营运汽车 1222 万辆，

---

❶ 四舍五入数据。

比上年末下降 0.8%。分结构看，拥有载客汽车 55.4 万辆、1647 万客位，比上年末分别下降 5.6% 和 5.9%；拥有载货汽车 1167 万辆、16967 万吨位，比上年末分别下降 0.6% 和 0.8%，其中普通货车 387.7 万辆、4716 万吨位，比上年末分别下降 4.7% 和 4.2%。

图 2-1　2017—2022 年公路营运汽车数量变化情况

中国汽车工业协会数据显示，2022 年全国汽车产量为 2702.1 万辆，比上年增长 3.6%，连续两年实现正增长。分结构看，乘用车产量 2383.6 万辆，比上年增长 11.2%；商用车产量 318.5 万辆，比上年下降 31.9%。商用车中，客车产量 40.7 万辆，比上年下降 19.9%；货车产量 277.8 万辆，比上年下降 33.4%。

（3）**水路**。截至 2022 年末，全国拥有水上运输船舶 12.2 万艘，比上年末下降 3.2%，净载重量 29776 万吨，比上年末增长 4.7%，载客位 86.2 万客位，比上年末增长 0.5%，集装箱箱位 298.7 万标准箱，比上年末增长 3.6%。

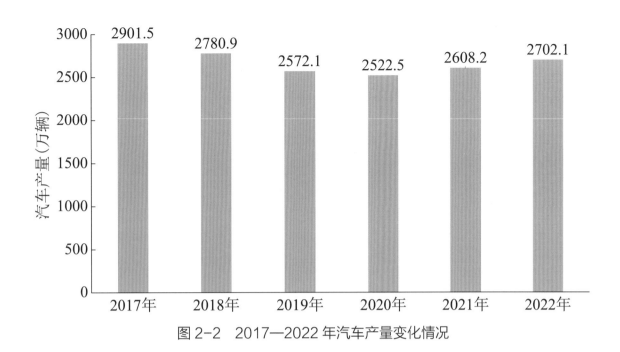

图 2-2　2017—2022 年汽车产量变化情况

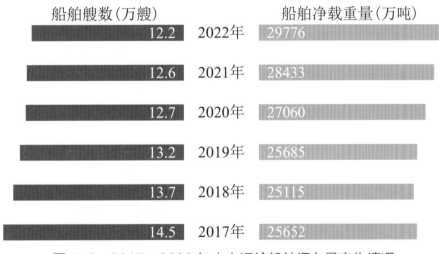

图 2-3　2017—2022 年水上运输船舶拥有量变化情况

中国船舶工业行业协会数据显示，2022 年全国造船完工量达 3786 万载重吨，比上年下降 4.6%，占全球总量的 47.3%，比上年提高 0.1 个百分点；承接新船订单 4552 万载重吨，比上年下降 32.1%，占全球总量的 55.2%，比上年提高 1.4 个百分点。截至 2022 年末，手持船舶订单 10557 万载重吨，比上年末增长 10.2%，占全球总量的 49.0%，比上年末提高 1.4 个百分点。

图 2-4　2017—2022 年造船完工量变化情况

（4）**民航**。截至 2022 年末，民航全行业运输飞机在册架数 4165 架，比上年末增加 111 架。其中客运飞机 3942 架，比上年末增加 86 架，占运输机队比重为 94.6%；货运飞机 223 架，比上年末增加 25 架，占运输机队比重为 5.4%。

图 2-5　2017—2022 年民航运输飞机在册架数变化情况

（5）**邮政**。截至 2022 年末，全行业拥有国内快递专用货机 161

架，比上年末增加 19 架。全行业拥有汽车 36.8 万辆，比上年末增加 1.9 万辆，其中快递服务汽车 26.5 万辆，比上年末增加 1.4 万辆。

（6）**城市客运**。截至 2022 年末，全国拥有城市公共汽电车 70.3 万辆，比上年末下降 0.9%。拥有城市轨道交通配属车辆 6.26 万辆，比上年末增长 9.2%。拥有巡游出租汽车 136.2 万辆，比上年末下降 2.1%。拥有城市客运轮渡船舶 183 艘，比上年末下降 6.6%。

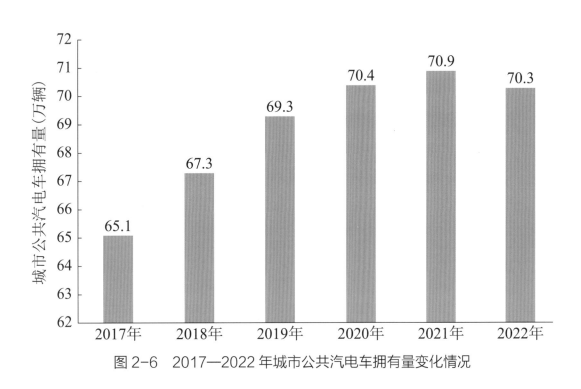

图 2-6　2017—2022 年城市公共汽电车拥有量变化情况

（二）
交通装备结构持续优化

（1）**交通装备绿色化**。截至 2022 年末，全国铁路电力机车 1.4

万台，占铁路机车比重为 64.3%，比上年末提高 0.3 个百分点。公路新能源营运货车 19653 辆，比上年末增加 8862 辆、增长 82.1%，新能源营运客车 29813 辆，比上年末增加 3799 辆、增长 14.6%❶。

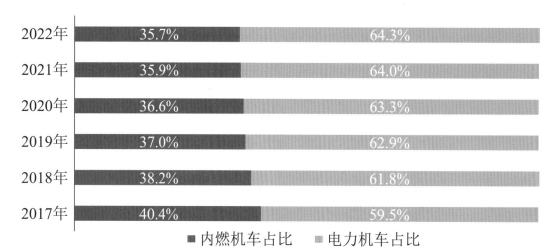

图 2-7　2017—2022 年铁路机车构成变化情况

截至 2022 年末，全国新能源公共汽电车、巡游出租汽车分别为 54.3 万辆和 30.0 万辆，比上年末分别增加 3.4 万辆和 9.2 万辆，占比分别为 77.2% 和 22.0%，比上年末分别提高 5.4 个 ❷ 和 7.1 个百分点。机场场内电动车辆占比超过 24%。中国汽车工业协会数据显示，全年全国新能源汽车产销分别完成 705.8 万辆和 688.7 万辆，比上年分别增长 96.9% 和 93.4%，连续 8 年保持全球首位，其中产量占全国汽车产量比重为 25.8%、比上年提高 12.2 个百分点。

（2）交通装备大型化。截至 2022 年末，全国载货汽车平均吨位 14.5 吨 / 辆，与上年末基本持平，大型营运载货汽车平均吨位提高至 21.8 吨 / 辆。全国水上运输船舶平均净载重量 2442.6 吨 / 艘，比上年末增

---

❶ 公路新能源营运货车、客车的统计口径为纯电动车和混合动力车。

❷ 四舍五入数据。

加 184.1 吨 / 艘、增长 8.2%。其中沿海船舶平均净载重量 8520.8 吨 / 艘，比上年末增加 362.1 吨 / 艘、增长 4.4%；内河船舶平均净载重量 1392.7 吨 / 艘，比上年末增加 100.7 吨 / 艘、增长 7.8%。全国集装箱船平均箱位数 1347.2 标箱 / 艘，比上年末增加 53.6 标箱 / 艘、增长 4.1%。

图 2-8　2017—2022 年新能源城市交通装备占比变化情况

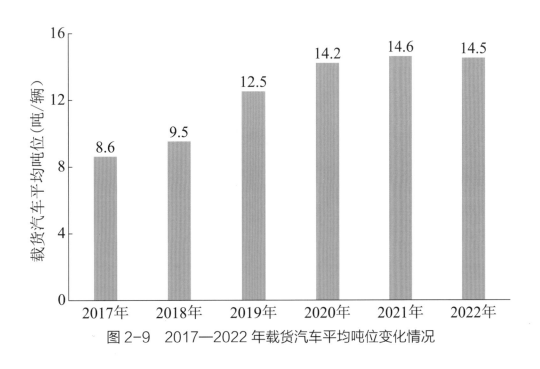

图 2-9　2017—2022 年载货汽车平均吨位变化情况

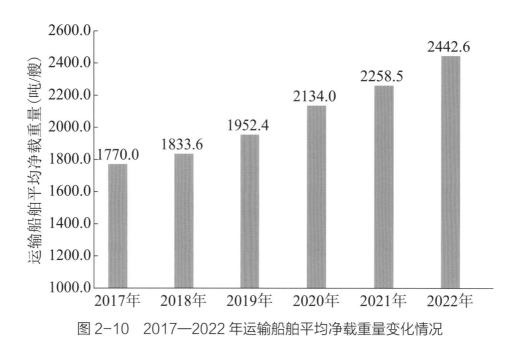

图 2-10　2017—2022 年运输船舶平均净载重量变化情况

（3）**交通装备专业化**。截至 2022 年末，全国拥有动车组 33554 辆，比上年末增加 333 辆，占铁路客车比重为 42.3%、比上年末提高 0.6 个百分点。多式联运等先进运输组织模式推广效果明显，公路牵引车、挂车及专用货车数量延续增长势头。全国拥有专用货车 63.4 万辆，比上年末增加 3.0 万辆、增长 5.0%；拥有牵引车 354.2 万辆，比上年末增加 7.5 万辆、增长 2.2%；拥有挂车 361.4 万辆，比上年末增加 2.1 万辆、增长 0.6%。

图 2-11　2017—2022 年动车组数量变化情况

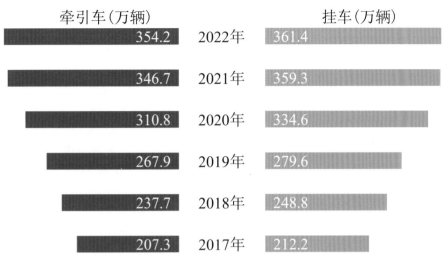

牵引车(万辆)　　　　　　　　　　挂车(万辆)

354.2	2022年	361.4
346.7	2021年	359.3
310.8	2020年	334.6
267.9	2019年	279.6
237.7	2018年	248.8
207.3	2017年	212.2

图 2-12　2017—2022 年公路牵引车、挂车数量变化情况

三、运输服务

2022 年，中国交通持续推进物流提质增效和出行服务品质提升，货运组织效率不断提高，客运服务便利化、无障碍化和适老化等便民惠民利民水平稳步提高。

（一）
交通物流保通保畅提高韧性成效显著

（1）持续完善制度机制。制定推进交通物流保障体系建设、交通物流运行动态监测管理等相关政策，持续健全突发事件情况下的交通物流保障体系，推动交通物流保通保畅工作长效化、制度化、规范化运行。因时因势调整优化交通物流保通保畅各项举措，围绕应急物资运输车辆通行证、应急物资中转调运站、司乘人员及重点产业链供应链"白名单"、货运枢纽场站集疏运等作出专项部署。建立实施日周月调度、挂图作战、电话转办、三级督办转办制度，坚持 7×24 小时值班值守和"一事一协调"，及时协调解决货车驾驶员电话反映问题。

（2）**强化对物流企业政策支持**。加强跟踪监测指导，全面落实第四季度收费公路货车通行费阶段性减免 10%、政府定价货物港务费降低 20% 等政策，有关港航企业主动减免库场使用费、滞箱费超 9 亿元，协调国产航油出厂价格阶段性让利、降低进销差价，降低企业燃油成本 33 亿元。推动出台减税退税降费、交通物流专项再贷款、贷款延期还本付息、社保缓缴等 40 余项涉交通运输业助企纾困政策，全年新增减税降费和退税缓税缓费超 4000 亿元。

（3）**保障重点物资运输顺畅**。全国累计保障各类重点物资运输需求 36 万余项。铁路深入实施电煤保供专项行动，全年完成电煤运量 14.9 亿吨，比上年增长 13%。做好"三夏"（夏收、夏种、夏管）生产期间全国免收联合收割机运输车辆通行费工作。水路运输实施"四优先"（优先过闸、优先引航、优先锚泊、优先靠离泊）措施，着力做好粮食、能源资源和化肥等运输保障。全力做好航空物流保通保畅，全年保障货运航班 26.7 万班。邮政行业全力保障医疗物资寄递，推动分拨中心和营业网点应开尽开，及时疏解积压邮件快件。

（4）**保障国际物流供应链总体稳定畅通**。铁路国际物流服务保障能力不断增强，中欧班列开行线路通达欧洲 25 个国家 200 多个城市，全年开行班列 1.6 万列、发送货物 160 万标箱，比上年分别增长 9% 和 10%。西部陆海新通道班列发送货物 75.6 万标箱，比上年增长 18.5%。全年完成国际道路运输超过 5000 万吨，比上年增长 20%。我国的全球海运连接度继续保持世界第一，国际海运运力保障能力不断增强，国际班轮公司优化重点航线运力投放，强化主要外贸集装箱航线运力保障。国际航空货运短板加快补齐，全年完成国际航线货邮运量 263.8 万吨。国际寄递物流服务网络不断拓宽，全年国际及港澳台快递业务量累计完成 20.2 亿件。

（二）
货运物流持续提质增效

（1）**货物运输规模有所下降。** 2022 年，全国完成营业性货运量 506.6 亿吨，比上年下降 3.1%；完成货物周转量 226161 亿吨公里，比上年增长 3.4%，增速较上年放缓 7.5 个百分点。2022 年，全国完成铁路货运量 49.8 亿吨，比上年增长 4.4%，其中集装箱发送量增长 22.2%；完成货物周转量 35946 亿吨公里，比上年增长 8.1%。

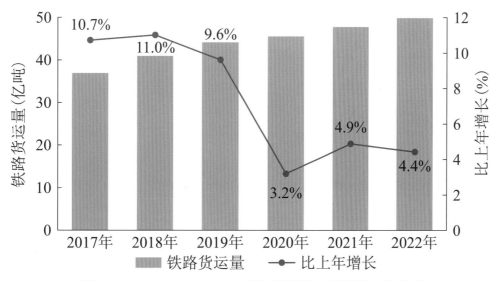

图 3-1　2017—2022 年铁路货运量及其增速变化情况

2022 年，全国完成公路营业性货运量 371.2 亿吨，比上年下降 5.5%；完成货物周转量 68958 亿吨公里，比上年下降 1.2%，高速公路货车流量比上年下降 10.4%。

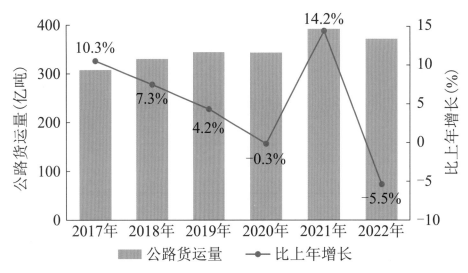

图 3-2　2017—2022 年公路货运量及其增速变化情况

2022 年，全国完成水路货运量 85.5 亿吨，比上年增长 3.8%，内贸货运船舶进出港艘次比上年下降 8.4%；完成货物周转量 121003 亿吨公里，比上年增长 4.7%。

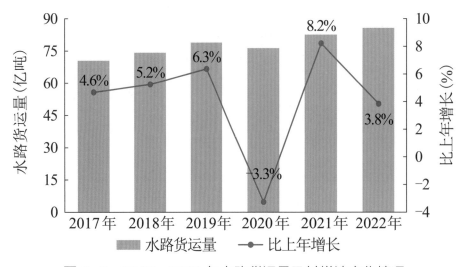

图 3-3　2017—2022 年水路货运量及其增速变化情况

2022 年，全国完成港口货物吞吐量 156.8 亿吨，比上年增长 0.9%，增速较上年放缓 5.9 个百分点。其中全年内贸货物吞吐量完成 110.8 亿吨，比上年增长 2.1%；外贸货物吞吐量完成 46.1 亿吨、比上年下降 1.9%。全年完成港口集装箱吞吐量 3.0 亿标箱，比上年增长 4.7%，增速较上年放缓 2.3 个百分点，其中内、外贸集装箱吞吐量分别完成 1.2 亿标箱和 1.7 亿标箱，比上年分别增长 3.6% 和 5.4%。环渤海港口群、长江三角洲港口群、东南沿海港口群、珠江三角洲港口群和西南沿海港口群分别完成货物吞吐量 44.6 亿吨、26.5 亿吨、7.1 亿吨、15.0 亿吨和 8.1 亿吨，比上年分别增长 2.9%、增长 3.0%、增长 3.2%、下降 3.8% 和下降 0.5%，五大港口群合计完成货物吞吐量 101.3 亿吨，占全国港口货物吞吐量的 64.6%。

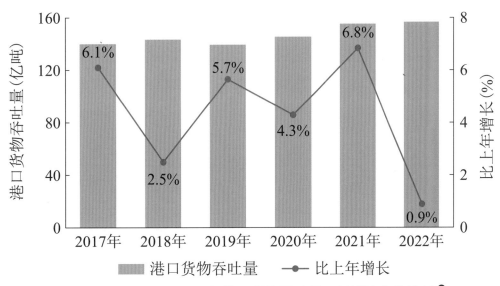

图 3-4 2017—2022 年港口货物吞吐量及其增速变化情况 ❶

---

❶ 2019 年起，港口统计口径调整为获得港口经营许可业户，增速按可比口径计算。

图 3-5　2017—2022 年港口集装箱吞吐量及其增速变化情况

2022 年，民航完成货邮运输量 608 万吨，比上年下降 17.0%，其中，国内、国际航线分别完成 344 万吨和 264 万吨，比上年分别下降 26.1% 和 1.1%；完成货邮周转量 254 亿吨公里，比上年下降 8.7%。

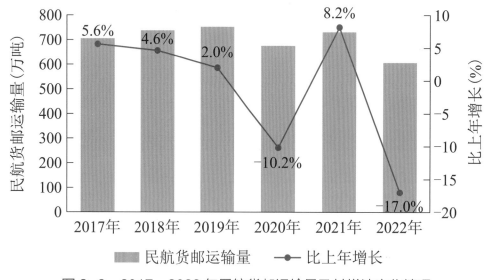

图 3-6　2017—2022 年民航货邮运输量及其增速变化情况

2022 年，全国邮政行业完成寄递业务量 1391 亿件，比上年增长 2.7%；完成快递业务量 1105.8 亿件，比上年增长 2.1%，其中同城、异地、国际港澳台业务量分别完成 128.0 亿件、957.7 亿件和 20.2 亿件，比上年分别下降 9.3%、增长 4.0% 和下降 4.1%。

图 3-7　2017—2022 年快递业务量及其增速变化情况

（2）**货运组织效率持续提升**。铁路货运服务持续提效，依托 95306 平台整体升级，推动"一个网站、一部手机、一次办结"全流程一站式服务，实现货运业务集中办理"全覆盖"，货运办理人均受理量、人均制单量分别增长 690% 和 450%。

道路货运持续转型升级，网络货运规范高效发展，全国 2537 家网络货运企业整合社会零散运力 594.3 万辆、驾驶员 522.4 万人，全年完成运单 9401.2 万单。推动承德、廊坊、盘锦、通化、连云港、宁波等第三批 31 个城市开展城市绿色货运配送示范工程创建工作，印发《城市绿色货运配送示范工程管理办法》，城市货运配送集约高效、绿色低碳发展步伐加快。持续做好农村物流服务品牌宣传推广工作。

航线网络布局持续优化，港口数字化转型不断加快，全年完成基于区块链的进口货物港口电子放货 68.3 万标箱，比上年增长 138%。钦州港自动化集装箱码头建成投产，全球首创"U"形堆场装卸工艺。

全国全货机数量提升至 215 架，占民航运输机队比重上升至 5.2%。运输保障效率不断提升，电子运单作业、特殊物资绿色通道、货车电子通行证、"单一窗口"等应用范围进一步拓展。

邮政普遍服务提质扩面，深入推进"快递进村"工程，全国 95% 的建制村实现快递服务覆盖，西部地区建制村周投递频次三次及以上的比例超过 99%。服务产业协同发展能力持续增强，全年累计培育年业务量超千万件快递服务现代农业金牌项目 117 个、邮政农特产品出村"一市一品"项目 822 个。快递服务满意度保持较高水平，服务全程时限、72 小时准时率、有效申诉率等指标全面提升。

实施国家综合货运枢纽补链强链，支持 15 个城市综合货运枢纽及集疏运体系建设，提升货物综合运输效率与质量，降低综合运输成本，支撑产业链供应链稳定。多式联运加快推进，开展第四批 46 个多式联运示范工程项目创建，示范线路进一步覆盖国家综合立体交通网主骨架和国家综合交通枢纽城市，示范工程全年完成集装箱多式联运量约 720 万标箱。指导推动集疏港铁路建设和"散改集"业务发展，全国港口全年完成集装箱铁水联运量 875 万标箱，比上年增长 16%。出台《关于加快推进冷链物流运输高质量发展的意见》，促进冷链物流运输畅通高效、智慧便捷、安全规范发展。

（三）
出行服务品质和包容性不断提高

（1）**旅客运输规模延续低位运行。**2022 年，全国完成营业性客运量 55.9 亿人，比上年下降 32.7%；完成旅客周转量 12922 亿人公里，比上年下降 34.6%。

2022 年，全国完成铁路客运量 16.7 亿人，比上年下降 35.9%，其中动车组客运量占比为 76.2%，比上年提高 2.6 个百分点；完成旅客周转量 6578 亿人公里，比上年下降 31.3%。

2022 年，全国完成公路营业性客运量 35.5 亿人，比上年下降 30.3%；完成旅客周转量 2408 亿人公里，比上年下降 33.7%。小客车出行方面，完成高速公路 9 座及以下小客车客运量 171.0 亿人，比上年下降 21.4%。

2022 年，全国完成水路客运量 1.2 亿人，比上年下降 28.8%；完成旅客周转量 22.6 亿人公里，比上年下降 31.7%。

2022 年，民航完成旅客运输量 2.52 亿人，比上年下降 42.9%，其中，国内、国际航线分别完成旅客运输量 2.50 亿人和 186 万人，比上年分别下降 43.1% 和增长 26.0%；完成旅客周转量 3914 亿人公里，比上年下降 40.1%。全年民航航班正班客座率平均为 66.6%，比上年降低 5.8 个百分点。

2022 年，全国完成城市客运量 755.1 亿人，比上年下降 24.0%。其中公共汽电车、城市轨道交通、巡游出租汽车、城市客运轮渡客运量分别为 353.4 亿人、193.1 亿人、208.2 亿人和 0.4 亿人，比上年分别下降 27.8%、18.6%、22.0% 和 11.7%。

（2）旅客运输服务品质持续提高。铁路部门精准实施"一日一图"，按需灵活安排运力，动态调整站车疫情防控措施，持续优化客运服务。修订《铁路旅客禁止、限制携带和托运物品目录》《铁路旅客车票实名制管理办法》，全面推广电子化补票，新型票制产品覆盖全路 380 个车站。开行"环西部火车游""新东方快车旅游专列""坐着火车游云南"等旅游专列。巩固拓展脱贫攻坚成果同乡村振兴有效衔接，持续开行公益性"慢火车"。

持续推动传统道路客运服务转型升级，加快新老业态融合发展，不断提升便民利民惠民服务水平。客运服务电子化程度进一步提升，全国二级以上客运站省域联网售票覆盖率达 98.8%，22 个省份实现部省联网售票服务，电子客票覆盖率达 90% 以上。制定实施《班车客运定制服务操作指南》，全国开通定制客运线路近 4800 条。制定出台《关于加快推进城乡道路客运与旅游融合发展的指导意见》，加快推进运游融合发展。

深化水路客运与旅游融合发展，加快推进 50 条水路旅游客运精品试点航线建设，京杭大运河北京通州城市段旅游航道建成运行，上海浦江游览、重庆两江游、福建闽江夜游等航线服务品质升级。邮轮码头布局加快完善，制定出台加快邮轮游艇装备及产业发展实施意见，青岛国际邮轮港区开发建设加速推进，湛江国际邮轮码头正式开工。

截至 2022 年末，全国客运航空公司共执行航班 239.4 万班次，平均航班正常率为 95.0%，高于上年 7 个百分点。全行业千万级以上机场近机位靠桥率为 79.0%，较上年提高 2.1 个百分点。民航服务质量监督平台功能不断完善，国内航空公司投诉响应率达 100%。41 家千万级大型机场开通旅客"易安检"服务，累计过检 40.3 万人次，平均过检时间缩减 38.7%。

截至 2022 年末，全国共有 53 个城市开通运营城市轨道交通，其中南通、黄石为新开通运营城市，城市轨道交通的连通性和便利性进一步增强。持续深入推进城市公共交通优先发展，深化国家公交都市建设，印发《国家公交都市建设示范工程管理办法》，全年完成对北京等 14 个国家公交都市建设示范城市动态评估和成都等 13 个国家公交都市创建验收，累计命名 46 个国家公交都市建设示范城市。在城市客运领域持续推广应用新能源车辆，新能源城市公交车占比达到 77.2%。

道路客运联网售票系统、重点水域电子船票系统建设提速，电子车票、船票普及率不断提高。铁路 12306 系统启动面向出行即服务（MaaS）的相关关键技术和产品研发工作。民航客票系统与铁路 12306 系统的合作范围不断扩大，继中国东方航空股份有限公司后，中国国际航空股份有限公司也与铁路部门合作实现客票系统的无缝对接和空铁联运客票的销售。持续完善 12328 交通运输服务监督电话系统功能，2022 年受理业务 2363.1 万件，限时办结率从 95.8% 提升至 97.5%，回访满意度率从 98.9% 提升至 99.7%。

全面完成 2022 年度适老化交通出行服务等 5 件更贴近民生实事，全年新增及更新低地板及低入口城市公共汽电车超过 3 万辆，打造 2700 余条敬老爱老服务城市公交线路，完成 9500 余个城市公共汽电车站台适老化改造，全国 120 余个地级及以上城市开通 95128 约车服务电话，近 300 个城市上线"一键叫车"服务，为 930 万余老年人乘客提供服务。全国 4000 余座地铁车站全部配备上下车无障碍渡板。高速公路服务区无障碍通道、车位、厕位基本实现全覆盖。

┤专栏 3-1├

国航国铁空铁联运产品

2022 年 12 月 27 日，中国国际航空股份有限公司与中国国家铁路集团有限公司举办"融合发展 畅行地空"国航与国铁合作暨空铁联运产品发布会，双方宣布推出全新国航国铁空铁联运产品。

此次上线的国航和国铁空铁联运产品共支持 30 个城市，50 个中转火车站，282 个通达火车站，覆盖北京、上海、广州、深圳、成都等重点枢纽城市。旅客可在"中国国航 App"和"铁路 12306App"一站式购买高铁与航班衔接的联运产品，实现"一次购票、一笔支付、一证通行"，极大提高旅客购票出行的全流程体验。

（四）
交通运输新业态健康发展

————————

　　截至 2022 年末，全国取得许可的网约车平台公司、驾驶员、车辆分别为 298 家、509 万人和 211.8 万辆，较上年分别增长 15.5%、28.9% 和 35.9%。受新型冠状病毒感染疫情等因素影响，全年完成 69.7 亿订单，较上年减少 16.3%。在 460 余个城市投放运营互联网租赁自行车，在营车辆 1500 万余辆，日均订单量约 3300 万单。

四、开放合作

中国交通坚持与世界相交、与时代相通，成立中国国际可持续交通创新和知识中心，持续深化与有关国家在交通运输领域互利合作，积极参与全球交通治理，切实履行国际责任与义务，服务构建人类命运共同体。

（一）
"一带一路"交通互联互通深入推进

中俄首座跨江铁路大桥同江—下列宁斯阔耶铁路桥正式通车、中俄黑河—布拉戈维申斯克公路桥实现通车运营，中巴经济走廊瓜达尔港东湾快速路竣工通车，中老铁路通车安全稳定运营满一周年，"澜湄快线"国际货物列车实现常态化开行。匈塞铁路贝诺段开通运营，印尼雅万高铁首次试验运行取得圆满成功。中欧班列持续健康发展，截至 2022 年末，中欧班列累计开行 6.5 万列、发送 604 万标箱、开通运行线路 82 条，通达欧洲 25 个国家的 200 多个城市，基本形成了对亚欧地区全覆盖的交通物流网络。

中国国际道路运输协定体系不断完善，合作范围拓展至 21 个国家，中国内陆城市与欧洲主要国家间国际公路运输（TIR）时间缩短至 2 周左右，运输便利化程度稳步提升。中越等国际道路运输线路常态化开行，国际道路运输通道进一步畅通。

中国水路国际运输航线已覆盖 100 多个国家和地区，海运服务覆盖"一带一路"沿线所有沿海国家。截至 2022 年末，中国已与 27 个"一带一路"沿线国家签订单边、双边船员证书承认协议。中国参与经营的希腊比雷埃夫斯港、斯里兰卡科伦坡港等港口运营良好。

中国与 101 个"一带一路"共建国家签署双边航空运输协定，与 64 个国家保持定期客货运通航。

中国邮政快递业务通达全球 220 多个国家和地区。

┤专栏 4-1├

中老铁路：区域互联互通、共同发展的样本典范

2022 年 12 月 2 日，中老铁路开通运营一周年，作为高质量共建"一带一路"的标志性工程，中老铁路开通首年累计发送旅客 850 万人次、发送货物 1120 万吨，其中跨境货物超 190 万吨，交出亮眼"成绩单"。

中老铁路全长 1035 公里，连接中国云南昆明和老挝首都万象，中老铁路开通以来，铁路部门创新"中老铁路＋中欧班列""中老铁路＋西部陆海新通道班列"等运输组织模式，开行中老铁路"澜湄快线"国际货运列车，增强了中老铁路辐射效应和跨境货运能力。

中老铁路改善了老挝的交通基础设施条件，提高了当地运输效率和水平，极大地改变了老挝的交通运输格局，有效打通了老挝的经济动脉。中老铁路的开通有利于包括老挝在内的中南半岛国家与中国互联互通，带动沿线旅游、商贸发展，共同打造政治互信、经济融合、文化包容的命运共同体。

（二）
交通运输国际交流合作持续深化

中国持续深化与相关组织、国家和地区在交通领域的政策对话，成功主办首届中（国）拉（共体）交通合作论坛、2022年中国航海日活动和北外滩国际航运论坛。加强跨国沟通协调，成功召开中老经济走廊交通合作工作组第一次会议、中缅经济走廊交通合作工作组第三次会议、中巴经济走廊交通基础设施工作组第九次会议、中德"内河航运和水路交通合作协议"第十七轮会议等重要会议，进一步强化合作共识。深耕厚植区域次区域合作平台，通过上海合作组织、中国—东盟（10+1）、中国—中东欧国家合作等区域合作机制，不断深化和扩大与有关国家（地区）交通运输合作与交流。与东盟在铁路公路基础设施建设、海运海事、航空运输等方面合作取得长足进展，与拉共体各成员国共同开展交通运输领域互利友好合作。积极参与国际公约和技术规则制修订，向国际海事组织（IMO）提交提案 114 份。进一步发挥在国际海运温室气体减排谈判中的引领作用，推动形成公正合理的减排方案，维护发展中国家共同利益。

┤ 专栏 4-2 ├

成功主办首届中国—拉共体交通合作论坛

2022 年 5 月 24 日，为落实中国—拉美和加勒比国家共同体（拉共体）论坛第三届部长级会议共识，中国交通运输部与拉共体轮值主席国阿根廷交通部共同主办首届中拉交通合作论坛，主题为"加强互联互通，促进可持续交通，服务中拉共同发展"。

中国交通运输部部长李小鹏和阿根廷交通部部长亚历克西斯·格雷拉出席会议并作主旨发言，拉共体其他 10 个成员国交通运输主管部门部长或代表出席会议并发言。

论坛通过了《首届中拉交通合作论坛部长联合声明（2022）》，宣布成立中拉交通合作论坛，对双方未来在论坛框架下以多种形式在铁路、公路、水运、航空、物流、海事等专业领域开展务实合作前景进行了展望，并明确第二届论坛于 2025 年举办。

（三）
中国国际可持续交通创新和知识中心成立

2022 年 10 月 14 日，中国国际可持续交通创新和知识中心成立揭牌仪式在北京举行。国家主席习近平向中心成立致贺信。中国国际可持续交通创新和知识中心是中国首个基于全球可持续交通发展的工作机构，是第二届联合国全球可持续交通大会的永久性成果，对促进全球交通合作、推动构建人类命运共同体具有重要意义。

┤ 专栏 4-3 ├

中国国际可持续交通创新和知识中心的主要行动

促进开放联动、互联互通。组织全球可持续交通高峰论坛等活动，创建可持续交通发展全球合作网络。

促进共同发展、公平普惠。打造全球交通发展的知识共享平台和成就展示平台。

促进创新驱动、增强发展动能。组建全球可持续交通创新联盟，促进全球智慧交通和智慧物流发展，推动大数据、互联网、人工智能、区块链等新技术与交通行业深度融合。

促进生态优先、绿色低碳。开展高端人文交流项目等，致力于加强全球绿色低碳交通能力建设，促进交通更加环保、出行更加低碳。

促进国际合作、应对全球挑战。建设全球可持续交通发展高端智库等，践行共商共建共享的全球治理观，为全球可持续交通发展合作提供智力支撑，进一步提高全球对可持续交通的认识和行动能力。

五、安全应急

中国交通坚持人民至上、生命至上，积极推动行业安全发展和高质量发展，着力防范化解交通运输领域重大风险，不断提升应急保障能力，为交通运输可持续发展提供坚实基础保障。

（一）
交通运输安全生产形势总体稳定

深入贯彻落实习近平总书记关于安全生产重要指示精神，紧紧围绕《交通强国建设纲要》《国家综合立体交通网规划纲要》和《"十四五"国家安全生产规划》设定的目标任务，保持高压严管态势，压实各方安全生产责任，加大重大风险防范化解力度，坚决遏制重特大事故，减少一般事故，降低事故总量。安全生产形势总体稳定，其中铁路领域，全年未发生特别重大、重大交通事故，铁路交通事故死亡人数比上年下降 14.6%；公路领域，全年未发生重特大事故，较大等级事故起数、死亡人数比上年分别下降 20% 和 30% 以上；水路领域，全年未发生特别重大事故，中国籍运输船舶事故❶起数、死亡（失踪）人数比上年分别下降 20% 和 40% 以上，港口未发生较大及以上等级事故；民航领域，运输航空百万架次重大事故率十年滚动值为 0.011，通用航空事故万架次率为 0.0367，运输航空严重征候万时率比上年下降 25.7%，人为责任原因征候万时率比上年下降 70.3%；邮政领域，全年未发生较大及以上等级安全生产责任事故，作业场地亡人事故比上年下降 71.4%。

（二）
交通运输安全监管进一步加强

（1）交通安全管理水平持续提升。强化安全生产制度保障，加强公路水运工程建设质量安全监管，持续推进交通运输安全生产标准化建设，印发公路水路关键信息基础设施安全规划，组织开展城市客运企业主要负责人和安全生产管理人员安全考核。继续做好百年品质工程创建示范工作。加大突出问题治理力度，依法查处非法营运客车、货车超限超载违法违规行为等，全年淘汰不合格常压液体危险货物罐车 1.7 万辆，变更适装介质罐车 2.0 万辆。截至 2022 年末，全国危险货物道路运输电子运单使用企业覆盖率达到 85.3%，

---

❶ 运输船舶事故包括造成人员死亡的事故和未造成人员死亡失踪的事故。

车辆覆盖率超过 66%。

（2）**安全生产重大风险防范化解不断深化**。初步建成交通运输安全生产重大风险"一张图"，全面排查安全生产重大风险 2800 余项。完成铁路沿线安全环境整治三年行动。实施干线公路安全设施精细化提升工程 21790 公里、灾害防治工程 5441 公里，完成公路危旧桥梁改造 13774 座，实施农村公路安全生命防护工程 13.5 万公里。完成安全生产专项整治三年行动，完成交通运输"百项整治任务"。民航开展发动机故障专项普查、优化中小机场和特殊复杂机场飞行程序等专项治理工作。深入开展城市轨道交通运营安全风险分级管控和隐患排查治理。

（3）**安全生产保障取得积极成效**。落实安全生产"十五条硬措施"，进一步强化安全生产责任落实，坚决防范遏制重特大事故。制定《进一步统筹发展和安全切实加强交通运输安全生产工作实施方案》等文件，全力保障北京冬奥会、冬残奥会等重大活动和重要节假日安全稳定。

（三）
应急保障能力持续提升

（1）**应急能力建设不断强化**。印发《交通运输部等二十三个部门和单位关于进一步加强海上搜救应急能力建设的意见》《交通运输部关于加强交通运输应急管理体系和能力建设的指导意见》等文件。

稳步推进国家区域性公路交通应急装备物资储备中心建设。组织开展海上搜救应急能力建设试点，成立南海第二救助飞行队，实现了海上伤病员直送医院，打通海上救助"最后一公里"，积极推动溢油应急设备库建设，稳步推进救捞船舶装备建造，12000 吨抬浮力打捞工程船（5 ~ 6 号）、80000 吨半潜式打捞工程船等交付列编，大型溢油回收船及配套溢油回收设备等项目稳步推进。成功举办北京冬奥会极端天气综合交通保障应急联动演练、2022 年国家海上搜救综合演练、中老缅泰澜沧江—湄公河水上联合搜救桌面推演，开展中美、中韩、中日搜救通信演习。北斗卫星导航系统加入国际中轨道卫星搜救系统，北斗报文服务系统加入全球海上遇险与安全系统（GMDSS）。

（2）突发事件应急处置响应及时有效。积极应对青海大通县山洪灾害、四川泸定 6.8 级地震等突发灾害，妥善处置"3·21"东航MU5735 航空器飞行事故、"6·4"D2809 次列车脱线事故、阳江"7·2""福景 001"起重船风灾事故、"9·18"贵州黔南州三荔高速重大道路交通事故等，做好防抗"轩岚诺""梅花"等台风工作，全力保障人民群众生命财产安全。2022 年，各级海上搜救中心开展搜救行动 1588 次，派出搜救船舶 12225 艘次、飞机 296 架次，成功救助遇险船舶 969 艘、遇险人员 9748 人，搜救成功率 96.4%。

┤专栏 5-1├

全国水上救助力量

截至 2022 年末，全国共计建成 24 处救助基地、3 处综合打捞基地、6 处飞行基地，拥有 70 余艘专业救助船舶、140 余艘打捞船舶、20 架救助航空器，建立 19 支应急救助队。目前，救捞应急保障力量在 9 级海况下能够出动，在 6 级海况下能够实施有效救助。

（四）
科学精准抓好疫情防控

按照"疫情要防住、经济要稳住、发展要安全"的要求，落实疫情防控各阶段方针策略、措施要求，因时因势调整优化防控举措，组织做好重点环节、高风险岗位人员疫情防控，全力阻断疫情传播，精准高效应对局部地区聚集性和散发性疫情，落实"乙类乙管"要求，科学精准抓好交通运输疫情防控，实现行业疫情防控平稳有序转段。

六、科技创新

中国交通坚持创新驱动，增强发展动能，大力推动大数据、互联网、人工智能等新技术与交通行业融合，科技成果和人才队伍建设取得积极进展，智慧交通快速发展，科技创新水平持续提升。

（一）
科技创新水平持续提升

———————

深化科技管理改革，强化科研机构使命导向和目标导向。加快推动交通科技创新，出台《交通领域科技创新中长期发展规划纲要（2021—2035 年）》《"十四五"交通领域科技创新规划》。"十四五"科技创新规划部署的关键核心技术攻关、智能交通先导应用试点和交通基础设施长期性能科学观测网建设等三项科技工程启动实施，4家综合交通运输理论行业重点实验室获认定，共有 323 项科技成果入选 2022 年度交通运输重大科技创新成果库，立项创建 7 项交通运输科技示范工程。科研设备保障能力持续增强，截至 2022 年末，公路水路交通运输领域科技活动重点单位拥有科研仪器设备 33.2 万台（套），比上年末增加 1.9 万台（套）、增长 6.2%。拥有价值 50 万元及以上科研仪器设备 5806 台（套），比上年末增加 350 台（套）、增长 6.4%，其中科学研究与技术服务事业单位、转制为企业的研究机构、高等院校、交通运输企业分别拥有 1459 台（套）、463 台（套）、1496 台（套）和 2347 台（套）。制定实施"一带一路"交通运输国际科技创新行动计划，国际科技合作空间进一步拓展。

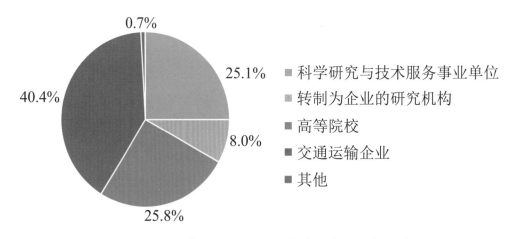

图 6-1　2022 年 50 万元及以上科研仪器设备占比

（二）
智慧交通发展取得新进展

（1）交通基础设施智能化建设扎实推进。 一批交通新基建应用场景逐步落地，杭绍甬智慧高速公路、广州港南沙港区四期工程、京杭运河智慧航道等重点项目加快实施。组织开展在役干线公路基础设施与安全应急数字化等专项行动及试点，推动覆盖644座公路长大桥梁结构健康监测系统建设，推进国家公路桥梁基础设施数据库汇总完善，覆盖32万座国家公路桥梁。建成苏州港太仓港区四期、钦州港大榄坪港区大榄坪南作业区7~8号泊位等一批自动化集装箱码头，截至2022年末累计建成14座自动化码头。完成长江干线数字航道综合服务平台建设，实现长江干线5400余座航标遥测遥控，160余个水文站遥测遥报，持续推进建筑信息模型（BIM）技术在长江航道整治等工程中的应用。

（2）交通装备智能化加速发展。新型复兴号高速综合检测列车创造了明线相对交会时速870公里世界纪录。C919大飞机开启验证飞行。持续开展自动驾驶技术推广应用，推动自动紧急制动、车道偏离预警、爆胎应急和胎压监测等辅助驾驶技术在道路运输车辆上的应用。中国首艘自主研发的油电混合智能拖轮正式启用，中国首艘120标箱纯电动内河集装箱船"江远百合"号下水，中国首艘两千吨级集散两用新能源运输船"东兴100"正式投运。

（3）运输服务智慧化水平持续提升。持续推进行业信息平台建设，印发国家综合交通运输信息平台实施方案。加大数据汇聚共享力度。推广"出行即服务"理念，提供城市公共交通实时出行信息服务，不断提高城市公共汽电车来车信息实时预报率和非现金支付比率。港航作业单证电子化和基于区块链的全球航运服务网络建设不断深化，2022年累计完成集装箱电子放货81.5万标箱，比上年末增长84.7%，制定实施基于区块链的进口干散货进出港业务电子平台建设指南。

（三）
人才队伍建设取得新成效

树立人才是第一资源理念，加快交通运输人才队伍建设。注重高水平科技人才培养，通过重大工程技术创新、重点项目研发锻炼人才，依托重点实验室及工程研究中心凝聚人才，加大青年科技人才支持培养力度，实施交通青年科技英才、行业科技创新人才推进计划，鼓励行业各类用人主体建立完善科技创新领军人才和团队支持保障机制。注重高技能人才培养，开展交通运输新职业开发和职业标准制修订，举办第十三届全国交通运输行业职业技能大赛全国总决赛，发挥职业技能竞赛引领作用，加强交通运输新业态从业人员保障，营造良好从业环境，培育规模宏大的知识型、技能型、创新型交通劳动者大军。注重高素质管理人才培养，组织开展能力素质提升培训，精准科学选人用人，大力培养选拔优秀年轻人才。交通运输人才队伍数量更加充足、素质更加优良、结构更加合理。

七、绿色发展

中国交通坚定不移走生态优先、绿色发展之路，把推动交通运输绿色低碳转型作为可持续交通发展的战略性任务，统筹推进碳达峰碳中和交通运输工作，为建设美丽中国贡献力量。

（一）
加强绿色低碳交通发展总体设计

持续完善交通运输领域绿色低碳总体设计，以交通运输全面绿色低碳转型为引领，以提升交通运输装备能效利用水平为基础，优化交通运输用能结构、提高交通运输组织效率，统筹推进交通运输行业绿色低碳发展。完善绿色低碳交通政策标准，印发 5 项环保标准，配合制定《国家碳达峰碳中和标准体系建设指南》。铁路绿色低碳发展取得新成效，全年单位运输工作量综合能耗控制在 4.15 吨标准煤/百万换算吨公里以内，比上年下降 1.2%。印发《公路水路行业绿色低碳发展行动方案》。持续开展绿色出行创建行动，北京等 97 个城市达到创建目标，绿色出行比例超过 70%，绿色出行服务满意率超过 80%。深入推进城市绿色货运配送示范工程。组织开展绿色出行宣传月和公共出行宣传周活动。

（二）
交通绿色低碳发展水平稳步提升

（1）**积极推动运输结构调整**。贯彻落实国务院办公厅《关于印发推进多式联运发展优化调整运输结构工作方案（2021—2025 年）》，加快大宗货物和中长距离货物运输"公转铁""公转水"，着力健全港区、园区集疏运体系，推动铁路专用线"进港区、进园区、进厂区"。完善多式联运骨干通道，加快货运枢纽布局建设，创新多式联运组织模式，加快推进多式联运"一单制""一箱制"发展。深入实施多式联运示范工程。截至 2022 年末，全国铁路、水路货物周转量占比分别达到 15.9% 和 53.5%，占比较上年分别提高 0.7 个和 0.5 个百分点。

（2）**持续推广绿色低碳交通设施装备**。截至 2022 年末，全国铁路电气化率达 73.8%。建成世界上数量最多、分布最广的充电基础设施网络，公共及私人充电基础设施数量达到 520 万台，比上年增长近 100%。截至 2022 年末，全国已建的 4145 个高速公路服务区建成充电桩 17581 个，其中新增配备充电桩的高速公路服务区 1043 个、新增充电桩 4207 个。换电站保有量增至 1973 座，较上年末增长 52%。截至 2022 年末，新能源城市公交车超过 54 万辆，新能源出租汽车近 30 万辆，新能源城市配送车辆超过 80 万辆。指导督促长江干线船舶 LNG 加注站运营，8 座 LNG 加注站全年加气 61 艘次、661.7 吨。支持广东省累计完成 100 余艘 LNG 动力船舶改造。长江经济带完成船舶岸电受电设施改造 5200 余艘，11 个省份港口和水上服务区全年使用岸电约 7497 万度，比上年增长 14%。渤海湾省际客滚船舶岸电使用取得重要进展，全年使用岸电 505 万度，比上年增长 3.8 倍。发布氢燃料电池动力船舶技术法规，推动电动船舶、甲醇动力船舶等示范应用。全国年旅客吞吐量超过 500 万人次以上机场飞机辅助动力装置（APU）替代设备实现"应装尽装、应用尽用"。开展快递绿色包装治理"9917"工程（到年底实现采购使用符合标准的包装材料比例达到 90%，规范包装操作比例达到 90%，可循环快递箱达到 1000 万个，回收复用瓦楞纸箱 7 亿个），稳妥推进可循环快递包装规模化应用试点。

（3）加快建设交通运输碳排放监测平台。按照"一张监测网、一套权威数、一个智能化核算预测体系和一体化管理"的目标，持续推进数据治理中心建设，汇聚运输装备、运输生产等 70 余类数据源。不断完善大数据分析中心建设，初步实现多源多维数据深度挖掘和融合分析。加快决策支持中心建设，实现多交通方式、多能源类型、多情景能耗和碳排放的精准核算及预测。推进全国船舶能耗中心建设，制定船舶能效技术要求，推进航运能效升级。

（4）进一步强化交通生态环境保护与修复。加快推进与生态保护红线相协调、与资源环境承载力相适应交通基础设施绿色发展模式，推动铁路公路统筹集约利用线位、桥位等通道资源，提高土地节约集约利用水平。进一步加强普通公路勘察设计和建设管理。深入推进《400 总吨以下内河船舶水污染防治管理办法》实施，巩固长江经济带船舶和港口污染防治行动成果、健全长效机制，实施定期调度通报制度。深化深圳、上海、浙江船舶大气污染物排放控制监测监管试验区建设。

八、交通治理

2022 年，中国交通重点领域改革持续深化，统一开放的交通运输市场加快建设，交通发展软实力稳步提升。

（一）
制度体系建设持续推进

有序开展《中华人民共和国铁路法》《城市公共交通条例》《农村公路条例》《中华人民共和国民用航空法》《民用航空器事故调查条例》等制修订工作，加快行业发展急需的规章立法进程，出台部门规章 42 件。修编发布《综合交通运输标准体系（2022 年）》。联合印发《交通运输智慧物流标准体系建设指南》，印发《绿色交通标准体系（2022 年）》《交通运输安全应急标准体系（2022 年）》，全年发布国家和行业标准 244 项。截至 2022 年末，交通运输行业现行标准共 3925 项，其中，国家标准 885 项，行业标准 3040 项。《铁路应用　轨道几何质量　第 1 部分：轨道几何及其质量描述》《智能运输系统　支持 ITS 服务的便携终端应用　第 2 部分：个人 ITS 基站与其他 ITS 基站之间数据交换的通用要求》等 7 项国际标准正式发布。中国成功当选万国邮联地理编码工作组主席国，主持万国邮联地理编码国际标准编制。发布《列控中心技术条件》《公路桥涵设计通用规范》《水运工程信息模型应用统一标准》等 31 项标准外文版。

（二）
重点领域改革不断深化

深化交通运输综合行政执法改革，机构撤并、职责整合、人员划转等改革任务全面完成。推动落实执法规范化长效机制，开展执法领域突出问题常态化查纠整改，实施执法队伍素质能力提升三年行动，推进严格规范公正文明执法。综合采用分路段、分车型、分时段、分出入口、分方向、分支付方式等形式推广高速公路差异化收费。截至 2022 年末，全国共 29 个省份（海南、西藏无收费公路）出台 250 项高速公路差异化收费政策。在海南省有序开展里程费改革试点工作。出租汽车行业发展更趋规范，完善违规行为处罚、联合监管机制、用户资金安全、运行数据管理、服务质量信誉考核等制度机制。从业人员权益保障不断强化，14 个省份出台了交通运输新业态从业人员权益保障工作方案，规范企业经营行为。持续探索推进职业伤害保障，北京、上海、重庆、四川、江苏、海南、广东等省（直辖市）探索网约车驾驶员职业伤害保障试点工作。交通运输新业态平台企业抽成"阳光行动"取得积极成效，全国各主要平台公司均已通过新闻媒体、App 等形式向社会主动公开计价规则和抽成比例上限。持续推进网约车行业健康发展，每月定期公开网约车行业运营、数据传输以及主要城市网约车合规化情况，约谈主要网约车平台公司，督促落实企业主体责任、依法规范经营。持续推进"司机之家"建设，切实改善货车司机停车休息环境，全国已累计建成并稳定运行 1300 余个"司机之家"。

（三）
统一开放的交通运输市场加快建设

推进落实行政许可事项清单管理工作，对交通运输领域 67 项行政许可事项制定实施规范，38 项部级行政许可事项制定办事指南。着力推进事前事中事后全领域全链条监管。推进"跨省通办"扩面增效，新增"航运公司符合证明查询核验"等一批政务服务事项纳入"跨省通办"事项。持续扩大道路运输电子证照应用服务范围，电子证照生成量达 539 万张。累计超过 815 万辆道路普通货运车辆通过线上方式办理年审业务，跨省大件运输许可由"网上办"转为"掌上办"。提升口岸通关效率，落实口岸收费目录清单制度。向全国复制推广"水铁空多式联运信息共享"等四项交通运输营商环境试点改革措施。推进实施延长货车在城市道路上通行时间等一批服务措施。优化网约车合规信息查询功能服务，累计为社会公众提供网约车合规化查询服务 810 万次。组织实施交通运输公共安全大数据平台工程，加快跨省非法营运、危险货物运输车辆违规经营等"互联网＋监管"试点应用。信用监管应用场景不断拓展，在信用承诺、信用评价、失信惩戒、"信易＋"、信用修复等方面开展创新实践，信用分级分类监管不断加强。联合出台交通物流领域金融支持政策，将交通物流专项再贷款政策延续至 2023 年 6 月底。全年交通运输业单位营业收入税费负担下降 15.4%。

（四）
交通文明程度稳步提升

聚焦物流保通保畅、"江河奔腾看中国""奋斗者·正青春"等重大主题宣传活动，讲好新时代交通故事。"奋进新时代"主题成就展全面展现了交通发展成就。大力弘扬交通精神，开展"感动交通年度人物""最美港航人""最美货车司机""最美海事人"推选宣传活动，做好冬奥会残奥会火炬手、IMO"海上特别勇敢奖"等交通人物宣传报道。持续开展"爱岗敬业明礼诚信"主题实践，深入开展文明交通绿色出行、"我的公交我的城"主题宣传，大力培树现代交通文明。积极发展科普基地，丰富国家科普资源建设，宁波中国港口博物馆、广州地铁博物馆、上海地铁博物馆、中国民航大学博物馆等 20 家基地成功入选第二批国家交通运输科普基地。

结 束 语

　　发展是人类社会的永恒主题。各国只有开放包容、互联互通，才能相互助力、互利共赢。作为最大的发展中国家，中国始终将自身发展置于人类发展的坐标系，以自身发展为世界发展创造新机遇。中国交通将坚持与世界相交、与时代相通，推动全球交通可持续发展、促进全球互联互通，服务保障全球物流供应链稳定畅通、推动世界经济发展，为推进全球发展倡议、落实联合国2030年可持续发展议程、推动构建人类命运共同体作出应有贡献。

本《报告》注释：

1. 香港、澳门特别行政区及台湾省统计数据未包括在本报告内。部分数据因四舍五入的原因，存在总计与分项合计不等的情况。

2. 公路营运汽车的统计范围是在公路运输管理部门注册登记的处于营运状态、最近年审日期在两年内的公路客运、货运车辆。

3. 营业性货物运输量为铁路、公路、水路、民航完成数，不包括管道数据。

4. 营业性旅客运输量为铁路、公路、水路、民航完成数，不包括城市客运数据。其中公路营业性客运量仅包含传统的班车包车客运量。

5. 本年公路客货运输量包括新疆生产建设兵团数据，全国增速按可比口径计算。

6. 报告中未注明出处数据来自交通运输部、国家铁路局、中国民用航空局、国家邮政局。

Report on the Sustainable Transport in China 2022

Jian Zhou   Xianjin Wang   Zandi Shang

China Communications Press Co., Ltd.

Beijing

Abstract

This Report comprehensively implements the guiding principle of the keynote speech delivered by Chinese President Xi Jinping at Opening Ceremony of the Second United Nations Global Sustainable Transport Conference. With focus on decisions and plans set forth in the *Outline for the Construction of the Country with Strong Transport Network* and the *Outline of the National Integrated Transport Network Plan,* in accordance with specific requirements of National Transportation Work Conference, this Report offers a panorama of eight aspects through analysis and research, namely, infrastructure, transport equipment, transport services, opening-up and cooperation, safety emergency response, scientific and technological innovation, green development, and transport governance. Systematic summary is carried out for the positive results in the sustainable development of Chinese transport industry in 2022.

This Report provides reference for transport authorities at all levels, macro decision-makers and all sectors of society to learn about and gain insights into the sustainable development of transport.

DRAFTING COMMITTEE

————————

Team leader：Jian Zhou

Members：

	Xianjin Wang	Zandi Shang	
Aoqing Lu	Qiannan Zhao	Cailiang Jiang	Zhongkui Li
Chunlin Tian	Geng Xiao	Xumei Chen	Yaping Kong
Zongwei Chen	Hong Geng	Wangxiong Wang	Zhang Cheng
Li Wu	Hongxu Liang	Ping Xu	Xuecheng Wang
Xianguang Wang	Gaiping Zhang	Wandi Zhang	Jialin Yao
Yamin Li	Xuan Chen	Jinying Yao	Jiayu Chen
Xuyong Hu	Yifan Huang	Meiying Sang	Wentao Fan
Lili Huang	Jianhua Chen	Jiandong Cao	Xiyuan Hu
Ruili Wu	Xiaozheng Zhang	Danyang Yu	Liuyang Liu
Jinsong Ye	Tao Wang	Xiaohui Duan	Chenggong Lin
Fenfen Qin	Na Liu	Na Wang	Tao He
Ruoqi Zhang	Xiaoli Song	Pengqi Li	Mengjie Zhou
Yuan Wang	Yuxi Zhang	Yijun Zhang	Wanshan Zhang
Yan Xia	Lei Zhou	Fengfeng Wang	Aiying Gao
Ruijun Ma	Qiong Li	Tiantian Su	Zilong Cao
Wanjiao Wang	Kai Luo	Aiyan Zhou	Yanxia Li
Ping Wu	Tiantian Zhang	Weiqing Zheng	Luyang Gong
Qingge Pang	Chao Yan	Chen Zhang	Xin Liu
Senyao Zhang	Mingwen Wang	Xin Zhao	Tingting Nie
Chang Liu	Shen Zhao	Xiaofei Liu	Xuexin Liu
Xinzhu Xiong	Jianhua Peng	Ruinan Jiang	Rujun Wang

PREFACE

The year 2022 was not only of extremely importance in the history of the Communist Party of China (CPC) and the People's Republic of China (PRC), but also witnessed a crucial step in China's transport development.

In 2022, the successful 20th CPC National Congress has drawn a magnificent blueprint for building a modern socialist country in an all-round way and comprehensively promoting the great rejuvenation of the Chinese Nation through a Chinese path to modernization. *The Report to the 20th National Congress of the Communist Party of China* not only stresses the necessity to develop China into a country with great transport strength at a faster pace, but also makes arrangements for building a modern infrastructure system as well as an efficient and unimpeded circulation system, reducing logistics costs, making faster progress in adjustment and optimization of transport structure, advancing clean and low-carbon energy transition in the transport sector, stepping up the construction of major infrastructure security system, promoting high-quality development under the "Belt and Road" Initiative and other transport-related tasks, thereby making clear the strategic directions and key contents of sustainable transport development at present and in the near future.

In 2022, Chinese President Xi Jinping sent a congratulatory letter on the establishment of the Global Sustainable Transport Innovation and Knowledge Center (GSTIKC), which pointed out: "Promoting sustainable development of global transport and facilitating connectivity among countries are of great significance for ensuring the stability and smooth flow of global logistics supply chains and boosting the development of world economy. The establishment of GSTIKC is an important move to support implementation of the UN 2030 Agenda for Sustainable Development. China is willing to work with other countries to make full use of GSTIKC as a platform to promote global transport cooperation, and contribute to advancing the Global Development Initiative, putting the UN 2030 Agenda for Sustainable Development into practice, and building a community with a shared future for mankind" . This shows the way forward and injects strong impetus into sustainable transport development.

The year 2022 marked the 10th anniversary of the new era of socialism with Chinese characteristics. The world's largest high-speed railway network, highway network, postal express delivery network and world-class port cluster sprang up like mushrooms in China. For many years, China ranked among the best in terms of major indicators, such as passenger and cargo transport volume and turnover volume of railway, highway, waterway and civil aviation, port cargo throughput and express delivery volume. Safe, smart and green transport was on a fast track. The construction of multi-dimensional, all-round and multi-tiered transport connectivity network along the "Belt and Road" was under way at a faster pace. In full blast, CHINA RAILWAY Express, ocean-going cargo vessels and cargo flights escorted the stability and smooth flow of the global industrial and supply chains, which convincingly contributed to writing a new chapter on sustainable development featuring connectivity of infrastructure, unfettered flows of trade and investment, and interactions between civilizations.

In 2022, Chinese transport industry holistically, accurately and comprehensively gave shape to the new thinking on development, did its best to accelerate the construction of new development pattern, vigorously promoted high-quality development, spared no effort to ensure the smooth and unimpeded flow of transport and logistics, held firm to transport work safety, proactively and steadily added effective investment in transport, took multiple measures for enterprise bailouts, and accelerated the construction of high-quality, comprehensive and three-dimensional transport networks. The quality of comprehensive transport services was continuously improved, the capacity for scientific and technological innovation in transport was further enhanced, the development of green and low-carbon transport was steadily boosted, the improvement of transport governance at higher level was accelerated, and the opening-up and cooperation went further in transport sector. Bigger strides were made to resolutely build China into a country with great transport strength. Transport sector strived to set the pace for Chinese-style Modernization.

In 2022, China stuck on the promising "Path to Sustainable Transport" and went all out to implement Chinese President Xi Jinping's call to "uphold open interplay and enhance connectivity; uphold common development and promote fairness and inclusiveness; uphold an innovation-driven approach and create more drivers for development; uphold ecological conservation as a priority and pursue green and low-carbon development; uphold multilateralism and improve global governance" at Opening Ceremony of the Second United Nations Global Sustainable Transport Conference. China gave full play to the role of transport as the artery of the economy and a bond between civilizations, worked with other countries to build a modern and comprehensive transport system featuring safety, convenience, efficiency, green style and economical benefit, constantly enhanced inclusiveness and resilience of transport, ensure easier movement of people and smoother flow of goods, and made steady progress on the way to sustainable development.

On September 25-26, 2023, the 2023 Global Sustainable Transport Forum (2023) will be held in Beijing. To demonstrate the latest progress in China's sustainable transport and share China's practices in the field of sustainable transport development, the *Report on the Sustainable Transport in China 2022* is compiled by China Academy of Transportation Sciences. This Report offers a panorama of eight aspects including infrastructure, transport equipment, transport services, opening-up and cooperation, safety emergency response, scientific and technological innovation, green development, and transport governance, with an aim to support the 2023 Global Sustainable Transport Forum (2023).

Author

September 2023

CONTENTS

I. Infrastructure

In 2022, China moderately devoted to transport infrastructure construction under forward-looking approach, accelerated the construction of a modern high-quality integrated multi-dimensional transportation network, optimized the layout, structure, function and system integration, vigorously added effective investment in transport, and strived to achieve effective improvement in quality and reasonable growth in quantity.

(I) Sustained Improvement of Integrated Multi-Dimensional Transportation Network

China constantly made progress in the construction of integrated multi-dimensional transportation network. The total mileage of integrated transport network reached more than 6 million km. The main framework space pattern of a national-wide integrated multi-dimensional transportation network, with

"Six Axes, Seven Corridors and Eight Passages" at the core, largely came into shape. The improvement of integrated transport hub system moved faster.

1. Extensive coverage of the railway network continuously expanded. By the end of 2022, China's railway operating mileage reached 155,000 km, an increase of 4,000 km compared with that in the late 2021. Specifically, the national railway operating mileage was 134,000 km, with railway network density reached 161.1 km/10,000 km², an increase of 4.4 km/10,000 km² compared with that in the late 2021. The double track rate and electrification rate of railway were 59.6% and 73.8%, respectively. The operating mileage of nationwide high-speed railways reached 42,000 km, an increase of about 2,000 km compared with that in the late 2021. Construction work commenced for Sichuan-Tibet Railway. Beijing Fengtai Railway Station (the largest railway hub passenger station in Asia), Zhengzhou-Chongqing High-speed Railway, Yiyang-Changsha Section of Chongqing-Xiamen High-speed Railway and Huzhou-Hangzhou Section of Hefei-Hangzhou High-speed Railway were put into operation. The construction of railway network, characterized by "Eight Horizontal and Eight Vertical Passages", quickened the pace.

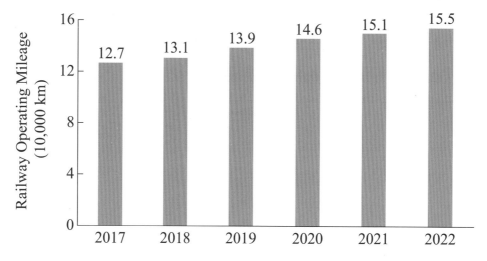

Figure 1-1: Changes in Railway Operating Mileage from 2017 to 2022

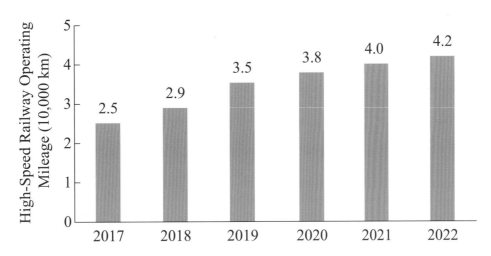

Figure 1-2: Changes in High-Speed Railway Operating Mileage from 2017 to 2022

Panel 1-1: Beijing Fengtai Railway Station was opened to traffic and went into operation

Built in 1895, Beijing Fengtai Railway Station has a long history. In 2010, its passenger service was suspended. Subsequently, renovation and expansion project started in 2018. After four-year renovation and expansion, Beijing Fengtai Railway Station has taken a new look since June 2022.

Beijing Fengtai Railway Station is China's first super-large railway station to adopt the design of double-deck railway yards for high-speed and ordinary-speed passenger traffic, where a three-dimensional traffic mode of "high-speed railway on the top, ordinary-speed railway on the ground, and subway under the ground" prevails, effectively saving land. A non-interfering passenger flow line system in station buildings is convenient for passenger transit. It can simultaneously accommodate up to 14,000 persons per hour. With 32 arrival and departure lines and 32 passenger station platforms, Beijing Fengtai Railway Station is the largest railway hub passenger station in Asia.

2. Internet proficiency of the highway infrastructure further enhanced.
By the end of 2022, China had a total of 5.355 million km of highways, an increase of 74,000 km compared with that in the late 2021. The highway density was 55.8 km/100 km^2, an increase of 0.8 km/100 km^2 compared with that in the late 2021. The total length of expressways reached totaled 177,000 km, an increase of 8,000 km compared with that in the late 2021. Specifically, the total mileage of national expressways reached 120,000 km, an increase of 3,000 km compared with that in the late 2021. The total mileage of highways of grade II and above reached 744,000 km in China, an increase of 20,000 km compared with that in the late 2021, accounting for 13.9% of the total length of nationwide highways, up 0.2%. By administrative level, the total mileages of national highways and provincial highways reached 380,000 km and 394,000 km, respectively. The total mileage of rural highways reached 4.531 million km, including 700,000 km of county roads, 1.243 million km of township roads and 2.589 million km of village roads. In China, 1.033 million highway bridges reached 85.765 million linear meters in total, an increase of 72,000 and 11.963 million linear meters respectively compared with those in the late 2021. 24,850 highway tunnels reached 26.784 million linear meters, an increase of 1,582 and 2.085 million linear meters respectively compared with those in the late 2021. The construction of key projects continued in full swing. Two national expressway trunks: G15 Shenyang-Haikou Expressway and G55 Erenhot-Guangzhou Expressway, as well as G1523 Ningbo-Dongguan Expressway and many other national expressway connections, were wholly completed. Several key engineering milestones of Shenzhen-Zhongshan Bridge were completed, and the construction project of Zhangjiagang-Jingjiang-Rugao Yangtze River Bridge has commenced.

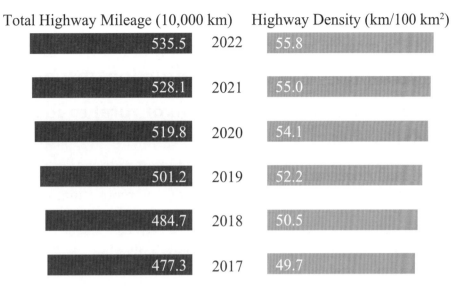

Figure 1-3: Changes in Total Highway Mileage and Highway Density from 2017 to 2022

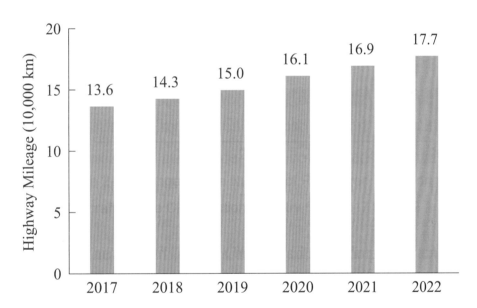

Figure 1-4: Changes in Highway Mileage from 2017 to 2022

Panel 1-2: Support the "Five Major Projects" for rural revitalization through the "construction, management, maintenance and operation of rural roads"

In 2022, transport authorities and competent authorities planned and launched a new round of rural road construction and renovation, with focus on the "Construction, Management, Maintenance and Operation of Rural Roads" to support the "Five Major Projects" for rural revitalization.

1. Backbone Road Network Upgrading Project: Accelerating the construction of fast backbone rural roads in towns, townships and major economic nodes, carrying out the renovation of old roads and the widening of narrow rural roads (or the construction of turnout lanes) in an orderly manner, intensifying the connection of rural roads with trunk roads, urban roads and other modes of transport, making more efforts for the construction of rural roads in old revolutionary base areas, ethnic minority areas, border areas, underdeveloped areas and reclaimed forest areas.

2. Basic Road Network Extension and Improvement Project: Letting more rural road construction projects be preferred by villages and households, propelling the construction of hardened roads in natural villages (villager groups) with large population size and natural villages along land boundaries in view of local conditions, implementing the construction of two-lane roads of incorporated villages in an orderly manner, making closer connections between inter-village roads and intra-village roads, planning and building the sections of rural roads crossing the villages while coordinating the function of main roads in the villages.

3. Security Capacity Improvement Project: Steadily taking actions to meticulously improve the management of highway safety facilities and traffic

order, constantly making progress in the demonstration project of "Safety Warning Flash Lights and Speed Bumps" for rural roads, exerting more efforts to identify and rectify hidden dangers of rural roads, bridges and tunnels, implementing and improving safety and life protection project of rural roads, and thoroughly reconstructing the old and dilapidated bridges.

4. Industrial Integration Development Project: Vigorously developing the mode of "Rural Road Plus", promoting deep integration of rural roads and industries, quickening the pace for the construction of rural industrial roads, tourism roads and resource roads, improving external road traffic conditions of major economic nodes in rural areas, and contributing to the development of rural industries.

5. Service Improvement Project: Placing priority over road sections for both transport and tourism purposes, improving service facilities along rural roads, effectively utilizing facilities such as passenger and cargo terminals as well as road maintenance squads in rural areas, expanding and developing service functions such as parking, charging, shopping, leisure and sightseeing, enabling high-quality development of rural roads with information technology, and enhancing service capacity and sustainable development capacity of rural roads.

3. Construction of modern water transport infrastructure network accelerated. By the end of 2022, China had 128,000 km of navigable mileage inland waterways, an increase of 326 km compared with that in the late 2021. Specifically, navigable mileage of inland graded waterways reached 68,000 km, accounting for 52.7% of the total mileage. Navigable mileage of inland waterways of grade III and above reached 14,800 km, accounting for 11.6% of the total mileage, up 0.2% compared with that in the late 2021. By river system, navigable mileage was respectively 64,818 km in the Yangtze River system, 16,880 km in the Pearl River system, 3,533 km in the Yellow River system, 8,211 km in the Heilongjiang River system, 1,423 km in the Beijing-Hangzhou Grand Canal, 1,973 km in the Minjiang River system and 17,610 km in the Huaihe River system. Construction started for the Pinglu Canal Traction Project, one of the backbone projects of China's New Western Land-Sea Corridor. Waterway regulation project for Qichun Waterway in the middle reaches of the Yangtze River was completed and accepted. Waterway regulation project for Jiangxinzhou-Wujiang River Section (Phase II) and other works ended with satisfactory results.

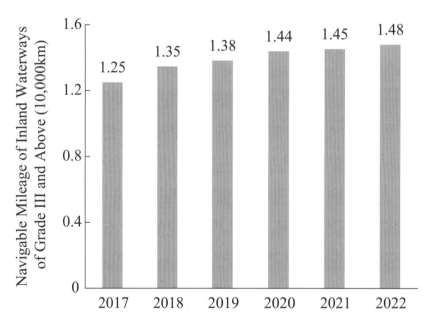

Figure 1-5: Changes in Navigable Mileage of Inland Waterways of Grade III and Above from 2017 to 2022

Panel 1-3: The Pinglu Canal Traction Project in support of China's New Western Land-Sea Corridor

The Pinglu Canal is not only a backbone project of China's New Western Land-Sea Corridor, but also a landmark project to develop China into a country with great transport strength at a faster pace. The Pinglu Canal starts from Pingtang River Estuary in Xijin Reservoir Area of Hengzhou City, Nanning, and flows into the Beibu Gulf along the Qinjiang River through Luwu Town, Lingshan County, Qinzhou City, with a total length of 134.2 km. This inland waterway is grade I and navigable to 5,000-ton-class vessels. The construction content of the Pinglu Canal includes waterway project, shipping hub project, river-crossing facilities along the waterway and supporting projects. Three double-line single-stage 5,000-ton-class ship locks (Madao, Qishi and Qingnian) will be established from upstream to downstream of the canal, with designed a total annual one-way through capacity of 89 million tons. The main parts are expected to be completed by the end of December 2026. Upon completion, the Pinglu Canal will become the shortest, the most economical and most convenient access to the sea in the Southwest China.

By the end of 2022, China had 21,323 production terminal berths in ports, an increase of 456 compared with that in the late 2021. There were 5,441 production terminal berths in coastal ports, an increase of 22 compared with that in the late 2021. There were 15,882 production terminal berths in inland ports, an increase of 434 compared with that in the late 2021. There were 2,751 berths of 10,000-ton-class and above, an increase of 92 compared with that in the late 2021. Specifically, there were 1,468 berths of 10,000-ton-class and above dedicated to coal, crude oil, metal ores and containers, an increase of 41 compared with that in the late 2021. Construction started for continental part of container terminal project on the north side of Xiaoyangshan. Major projects, such as Jiangsu Binhai LNG Terminal Project and Berths No. 8-9 of Lvsi Operation Area in Tongzhou Bay Port Area of Nantong Port, were completed.

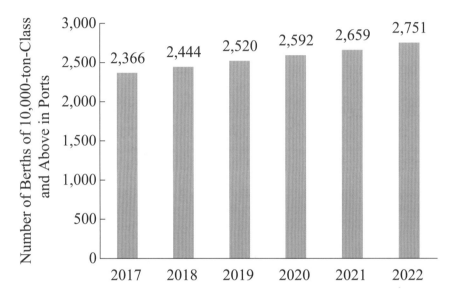

Figure 1-6: Changes in the Number of Berths of 10,000-ton-Class and Above in Ports from 2017 to 2022

4. Weak links of civil aviation infrastructure were constantly shored up. By the end of 2022, China had 254 certified civil air transport airports, an increase of six compared with that in the late 2021, including 253 airports for regular flights. There were 283 runways, 7,315 aircraft stands and 17.989 million m² of terminal area, respectively, an increase of seven, 182 and 110,000 m² compared with those in the late 2021. Ezhou Huahu Airport, the largest specialized cargo airport in Asia, was completed and put into operation. In Tibet, both Shannan Longzi Airport and Xigaze Dingri Airport were opened to traffic. Renovation and expansion project of Lhasa Kongga International Airport has commenced. In China, regular flights were available for 249 cities (or regions). Six cities (or regions) were additionally navigable to regular flights, i.e., Zhaosu County, Aral City and Tashkurgan Tajik Autonomous County in Xinjiang Uygur Autonomous Region, Ezhou City in Hubei Province, Shannan City and Xigaze City in Tibet Autonomous Region.

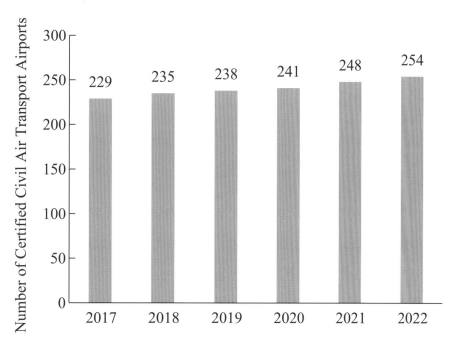

Figure 1-7: Changes in the Number of Certified Civil
Air Transport Airports from 2017 to 2022

5. Basic postal network structure continuously turned for the better. By the end of 2022, China had 44,000 postal routes, a decrease of 2,000 compared with that in the late 2021. Total length of one-way postal routes was 11.425 million km, down 503,000 km compared with that in the late 2021. There were 104,000 rural delivery routes and 119,000 urban delivery routes, respectively. There were 434,000 business outlets of various types in whole postal industry, an increase of 21,000 compared with that in the late 2021 (including 117,000 in rural areas, an increase of 1,000 compared with that in the late 2021). There were 231,000 express delivery service outlets, with an increase of 3,000❶ compared

---

❶ Rounded data.

with that in the late 2021 (including 76,000 in rural areas, with an increase of 1,000 compared with that in the late 2021). There were 212,000 express delivery service routes, an increase of 12,000 compared with that in the late 2021. Total length of one-way express delivery service routes was 48.704 million km, an increase of 5.648 million km compared with that in the late 2021.

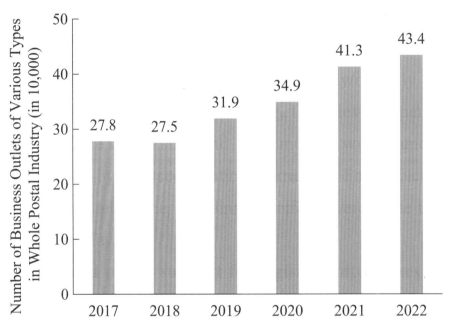

Figure 1-8: Changes in the Number of Business Outlets of Various Types in Whole Postal Industry from 2017 to 2022

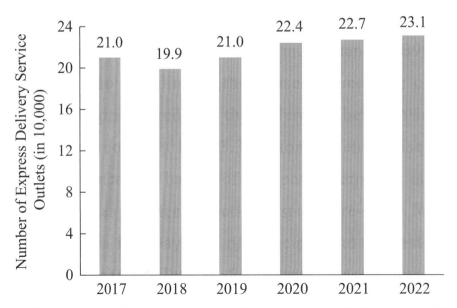

Figure 1-9: Changes in the Number of Express Delivery Service Outlets from 2017 to 2022

6. Steady progress was made in the development of urban transport facilities. By the end of 2022, China had urban bus lanes of 19,870 km, an increase of 1,607 km compared with that in the late 2021. China had 292 urban rail transit lines in operation, an increase of 17 compared with that in the late 2021. Total length of urban rail transit lines in operation was 9,555 km, an increase of 819 km compared with that in the late 2021. Specifically, there were 240 subway lines, reaching 8,448 km; and seven light rail lines, reaching 263 km. China had 78,020 urban public tram lines in operation, an increase of 2,250 compared with that in the late 2021. Total length of urban public tram lines in operation was 1.66 million km, an increase of 70,000 km compared with that in the late 2021. China had 79 urban passenger ferry routes in operation, a decrease of five compared with that in the late 2021. Total length of urban passenger ferry routes in operation was 334.6 km, a decrease of 41.7 km compared with that in the late 2021.

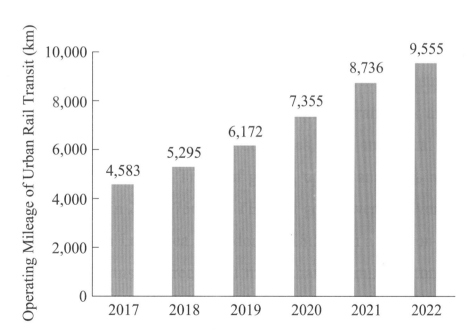

Figure 1-10: Changes in Operating Mileage of Urban Rail Transit from 2017 to 2022

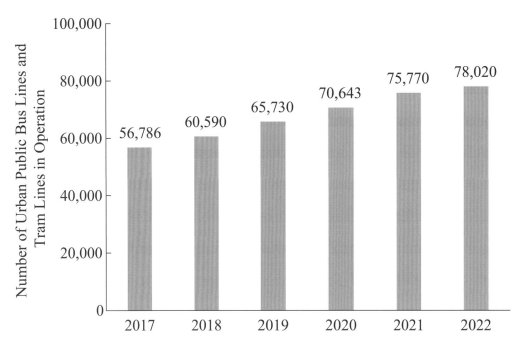

Figure 1-11: Changes in the Number of Urban Public Bus Lines and
Tram Lines in Operation from 2017 to 2022

(II) Huge Fixed Asset Investment in Transport

In 2022, the construction funds were earmarked for transport industry through multiple channels, while faster progress was made in the construction of major projects, making positive contributions to stabilizing the economic fundamentals. Fixed asset investment in transport amounted to RMB3.8545 trillion, up 6.4% on a year-on-year basis. Investment in highway, waterway and civil aviation amounted to RMB2.8527 trillion, RMB167.9 billion and RMB123.1 billion, up 9.7%, 10.9% and 0.7% compared with those in 2021, respectively. Investment in railway amounted to RMB710.9 billion, down 5.1% on a year-on-year basis. As for investment in highway construction, investment in expressways and general national and provincial highways increased by 7.3% and 6.5%, respectively. Driven by a new round of rural road construction and upgrading, investment in rural roads increased by 15.6% on a year-on-year basis.

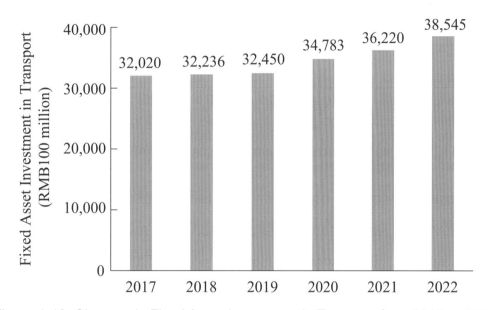

Figure 1-12: Changes in Fixed Asset Investment in Transport from 2017 to 2022

II. Transport Equipment

In 2022, China boasted stable transport equipment supply capacity on the whole, constantly optimized transport equipment mix with ever-increasing green and professional level.

(I) Stable Transport Equipment Supply Capacity on the Whole

1. Railways: By the end of 2022, China had 22,100[1] railway locomotives, including 7,800 diesel locomotives and 14,200 electric locomotives, which basically remained unchanged compared with that in the late 2021. China had 77,000 passenger trains, a decrease of 200 compared with that in the late 2021. China had 997,000 cargo trains, an increase of 31,000 compared with that in the late 2021. According to the data from

---

[1] Rounded data.

National Bureau of Statistics, China's railway locomotive output reached 1,463 in 2022, up 34.8% compared with that in the late 2021.

2. Highways: By the end of 2022, China had 12.22 million operating vehicles on highways, down 0.8% compared with that in the late 2021. By vehicle structure, there were 554,000 passenger vehicles and 16.47 million passenger seats, down 5.6% and 5.9% respectively compared with those in the late 2021. There were 11.67 million cargo vehicles, equal to 169.67 million tons, down 0.6% and 0.8% respectively compared with those in the late 2021. Specifically, there were 3.877 million general-purpose cargo vehicles, equal to 47.16 million tons, down 4.7% and 4.2% respectively compared with those in the late 2021.

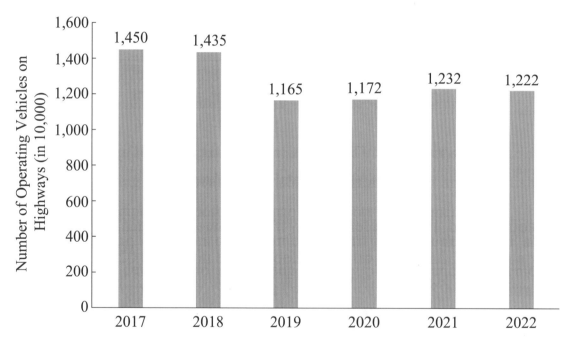

Figure 2-1: Changes in the Number of Operating Vehicles
on Highways from 2017 to 2022

According to the data from China Association of Automobile Manufacturers, China's automobile output was 27.021 million in 2022, up 3.6% compared with that in the late 2021 and on the increase for two consecutive years. By vehicle, the output of passenger automobiles was 23.836 million, up 11.2% on a year-on-year basis. The output of commercial automobiles was 3.185 million, down 31.9% on a year-on-year basis. Specifically, the outputs of passenger automobiles and cargo automobiles were 407,000 and 2.778 million, down 19.9% and 33.4% on a year-on-year basis, respectively.

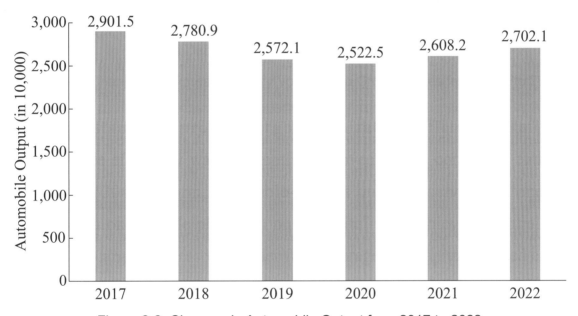

Figure 2-2: Changes in Automobile Output from 2017 to 2022

3. Waterways: By the end of 2022, China had 122,000 water transport vessels, down 3.2% compared with that in the late 2021. Net deadweight reached 297.76 million tons, up 4.7% compared with that in the late 2021. Passenger capacity reached 862,000, up 0.5% compared with that in the late 2021. Container capacity reached 2.987 million TEUs, up 3.6% compared with that in the late 2021.

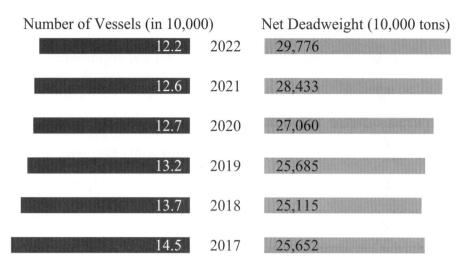

Figure 2-3: Changes in Waterway Transport Vessels from 2017 to 2022

According to the data from China Association of the National Shipbuilding Industry, shipbuilding completions reached 37.86 million DWT in 2022, down 4.6% on a year-on-year basis, accounting for 47.3% of the global total (0.1% higher than that in 2021). New ship orders reported 45.52 million DWT, down 32.1% on a year-on-year basis, accounting for 55.2% of the global total (1.4% higher than that in 2021). By the end of 2022, ship orders on hand reached 105.57 million DWT, up 10.2% compared with that in the late 2021, accounting for 49.0% of the global total (1.4% higher than that in the late 2021).

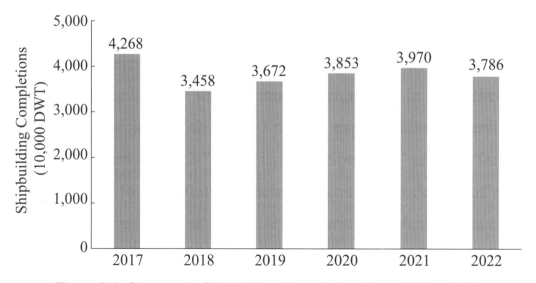

Figure 2-4: Changes in Shipbuilding Completions from 2017 to 2022

4. Civil aviation: By the end of 2022, China had 4,165 registered transport aircrafts in the civil aviation industry, an increase of 111 compared with that in the late 2021. Specifically, there were 3,942 passenger aircrafts, an increase of 86 compared with that in the late 2021, accounting for 94.6% of the transport fleet. There were 223 cargo aircrafts, an increase of 25 compared with that in the late 2021, accounting for 5.4% of the transport fleet.

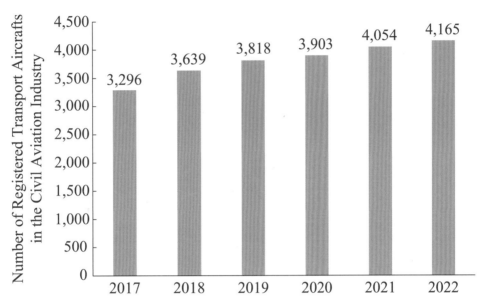

Figure 2-5: Changes in the Number of Registered Transport
Aircrafts in the Civil Aviation Industry from 2017 to 2022

5. Post: By the end of 2022, China had 161 domestic express cargo aircrafts in the post industry, an increase of 19 compared with that in the late 2021. China had 368,000 vehicles in the post industry, an increase of 19,000 compared with that in the late 2021 (including 265,000 express service vehicles, an increase of 14,000 compared with that in the late 2021).

6. Urban passenger transport: By the end of 2022, China had 703,000 urban public buses and trams, down 0.9% compared with that in the late

2021. There were 62,600 urban rail transit vehicles, up 9.2% compared with that in the late 2021. There were 1.362 million cruising taxis, down 2.1% compared with that in the late 2021. There were 183 urban passenger ferry ships, down 6.6% compared with that in the late 2021.

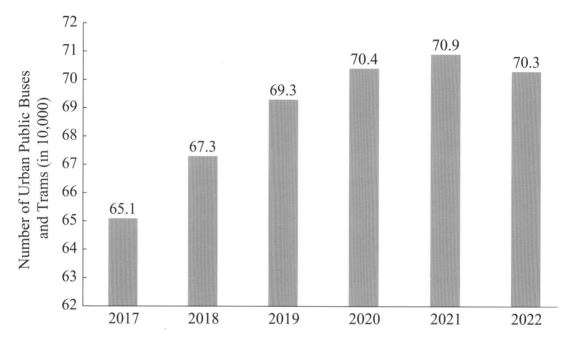

Figure 2-6: Changes in the Number of Urban Public Buses and Trams from 2017 to 2022

(II) Constantly Optimized Transport Equipment Mix

1. Green transport equipment: By the end of 2022, China had 14,000 railway electric locomotives, accounting for 64.3% of railway locomotives, up 0.3% compared with that in the late 2021; 19,653 operating new energy vehicles for cargo transport on highways, an increase of 8,862 or up 82.1% compared with that in the late 2021; and 29,813 new energy vehicles for passenger transport, an increase of 3,799 or up 14.6% compared with that in the late 2021.❶

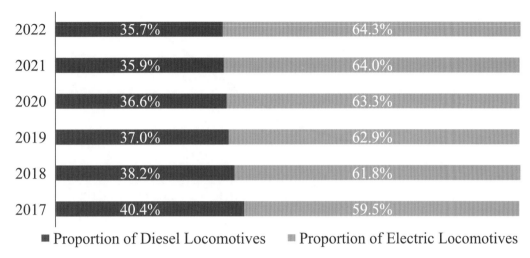

Figure 2-7: Changes in the Proportions of Various Types
of Railway Locomotives from 2017 to 2022

By the end of 2022, China had 543,000 new energy public buses and trams as well as 300,000 cruising taxis, an increase of 34,000 and 92,000 respectively compared with that in the late 2021, accounting for 77.2% and 22.0% respectively (5.4%❷ and 7.1% higher than those in the late 2021). Electric vehicles accounted for more than 24% in the airports. According to the data from China Association of Automobile Manufacturers, the annual new energy vehicle output and sales volume were 7.058 million and 6.887 million in China, up 96.9% and 93.4% respectively compared with those in the late 2021, ranking the first in the world for eight consecutive years. Specifically, new energy vehicle output accounted for 25.8% of the national automobile output, up 12.2% on a year-on-year basis.

---

❶ Statistical caliber of operating new energy vehicles for passenger and cargo transport on highways is applicable to pure electric vehicles and hybrid vehicles.

❷ Rounded data.

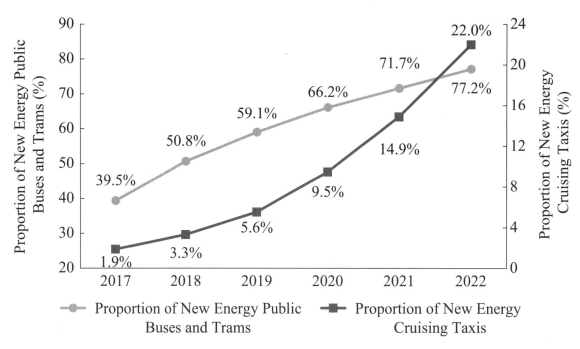

Figure 2-8: Changes in the Proportions of New Energy Vehicles
in Urban Transport Equipment from 2017 to 2022

2. Large-scale transport equipment: By the end of 2022, the average tonnage of cargo vehicles reached 14.5 tons/vehicle in China, which basically remained unchanged compared with that in the late 2021. The average tonnage of large-sized operating cargo vehicles increased to 21.8 tons/vehicle. The average net deadweight of water transport vessels was 2,442.6 tons/vessel, an increase of 184.1 tons/vessel or up 8.2% compared with that in the late 2021. Specifically, the average net deadweight of coastal vessels reached 8,520.8 tons/vessel, an increase of 362.1 tons/vessel or up 4.4% compared with that in the late 2021. The average net deadweight of inland vessels reached 1,392.7 tons/vessel, an increase of 100.7 tons/vessel or up 7.8% compared with that in the late 2021. The average container capacity of container vessel was 1,347.2 TEUs/vessel in China, an increase of 53.6 TEUs/vessel or up 4.1% compared with that in the late 2021.

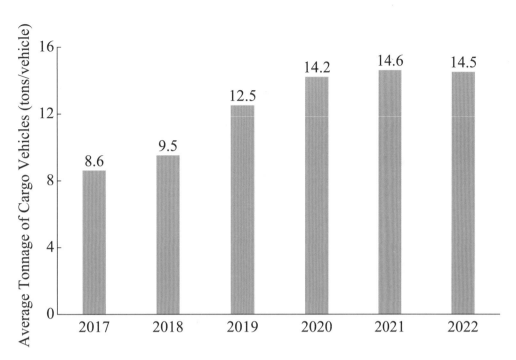

Figure 2-9: Changes in the Average Tonnage of Cargo Vehicles from 2017 to 2022

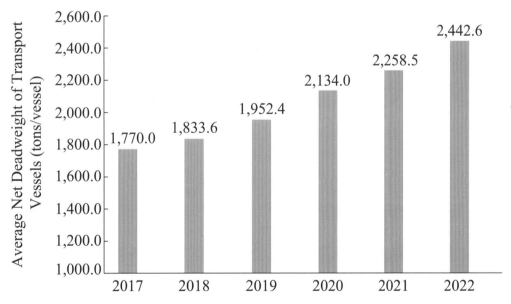

Figure 2-10: Changes in the Average Net Deadweight of
Transport Vessels from 2017 to 2022

3. Specialized traffic equipment: By the end of 2022, China had 33,554 electric multiple units, an increase of 333 compared with that in the late 2021, accounting for 42.3% of passenger trains, up 0.6% compared with that in the late 2021. Advanced transport organization modes, such as multi-modal transport, demonstrated remarkable promotion effect. Highway tractors, trailers and special-purpose cargo vehicles continuously increased. China had 634,000 special-purpose cargo vehicles, an increase of 30,000 or up 5.0% compared with that in the late 2021; 3.542 million tractors, an increase of 75,000 or up 2.2% compared with that in the late 2021; and 3.614 million trailers, an increase of 21,000 or up 0.6% compared with that in the late 2021.

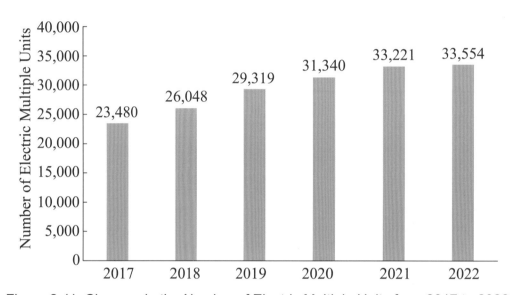

Figure 2-11: Changes in the Number of Electric Multiple Units from 2017 to 2022

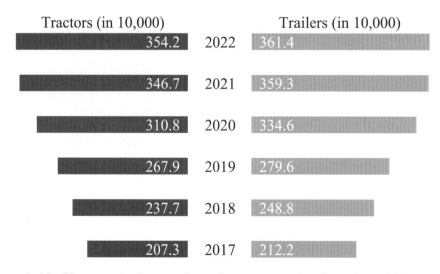

Figure 2-12: Changes in the number of tractors and trailers from 2017 to 2022

III. Transport Services

In 2022, Chinese transport sector constantly improved the quality and efficiency of logistics and the quality of trip services. Moreover, cargo transport organization became increasingly efficient; facilitated, barrier-free and elderly-oriented passenger transport services steadily progress towards convenient, useful and favorable for the people.

(I) Remarkable Results for Smooth and Unimpeded Flow and Higher Resilience of Transport and Logistics

1. Continuous improvement of systems and mechanisms: Relevant policies were introduced to promote the construction of transport and logistics support system and the dynamic monitoring and management of transport and logistics operation, constantly improved the transport and logistics support system in response to emergencies, and provided impetuses to the long-acting, institutionalized and standardized operation of smooth and unimpeded flow of transport and logistics. In view of changing circumstances in right time, various measures were adjusted and optimized to ensure the smooth and unimpeded flow of transport and logistics. Special arrangements were made for emergency materials transport vehicle permits, emergency materials transfer stations, "whitelists" for drivers, passengers and key industrial chains and supply chains, collection, distribution and transport via cargo hub terminals and stations and other aspects. Daily/weekly/monthly scheduling, wall chart operation, telephone forwarding, three-level supervision and transfer system were established and implemented with round-the-clock work shift and "case-by-case coordination" carried on. For problems reported by truck drivers via telephone, coordination efforts were made to solve the problems without delay.

2. Underpinned policy support for logistics enterprises: Tracking, monitoring and guidance were intensified. Policies, such as phased reduction of truck tolling on tollways by 10% and reduction of port fees for government-priced goods by 20%, were enforced in the fourth quarter. Relevant port and shipping enterprises took the initiative to reduce storage yard fees and container detention fees by more than RMB900 million. Relevant policy also coordinated the phased concession of domestic jet fuel ex-factory prices, reduced the difference between imports and sales, and cut fuel costs by RMB3.3 billion for enterprises. Over 40 policies were introduced for bailout of transport enterprises, including tax reduction, tax rebates and fee reductions, special re-loans for transport and logistics, delays in repayment of principle and interest and social security payment deferrals. Tax and fee reductions as well as tax rebates amounted to more than RMB400 billion throughout the year.

3. Unfretted transport of key materials: Over 360,000 transport demands of key materials were satisfied in China. The railway industry launched a special campaign to ensure the thermal coal supply and transported 1.49 billion tons of thermal coal in 2022, up 13% on a year-on-year basis. During the production period of summer harvest, summer planting and summer field management, combine harvester transport vehicles were exempted from the tolls all over the country. "Four Priorities" (priority lockage, priority pilotage, priority anchoring and priority berthing and unberthing) were given for waterway transport. Transport support was provided for foodstuff, energy resources and fertilizers. Every effort was made to ensure the smooth and unimpeded flow of aviation logistics, and services were rendered for 267,000 cargo flights in 2022. Post industry spared no effort to ensure the delivery of medical supplies, opening distribution centers and business outlets in service as much as possible to promptly handle the backlogging mails and express items.

4. Overall stability and smooth flow of international logistics supply chain: Capabilities of international railway logistics service support were constantly enhanced. "CHINA RAILWAY Express" ran back and forth in more than 200 cities in 25 European countries, with an annual volume of 16,000 trains and 1.6 million TEUs of goods, up 9% and 10% respectively compared with those in 2021. 756,000 TEUs of goods were delivered through China's New Western Land-Sea Corridor, up 18.5% on a year-on-year basis. International road transport recorded more than 50 million tons, up 20% on a year-on-year basis. China remained No. 1 in terms of international shipping connectivity and presented increasingly stronger ability to support international shipping capacity. Liner multinationals optimized the transport capacity layout for key routes and placed transport capacity for major foreign trade container routes. China stepped up efforts to fill the gaps in international air cargo transport. The annual cargo and mail transport on international routes reached 2.638 million tons. The international delivery logistics service network was continuously expanded. 2.02 billion express deliveries were made to other countries and regions including Hong Kong, Macao and Taiwan in 2022.

(II) Continuous Improvement of the Quality and Efficiency of Cargo Logistics

1. The scale of cargo transport declined: In 2022, China's commercial cargo transport volume reached 50.66 billion tons, down 3.1% on a year-on-year basis. Turnover volume of cargo traffic reached 22.6161 trillion ton-kilometers, up 3.4% on a year-on-year basis, with a growth rate 7.5% lower than that in 2021. In 2022, China's railway cargo volume reached 4.98 billion tons, up 4.4% on a year-on-year basis. Specifically, container shipments increased by 22.2%, and turnover volume of container traffic reached 3.5946 trillion ton-kilometers, up 8.1% on a year-on-year basis.

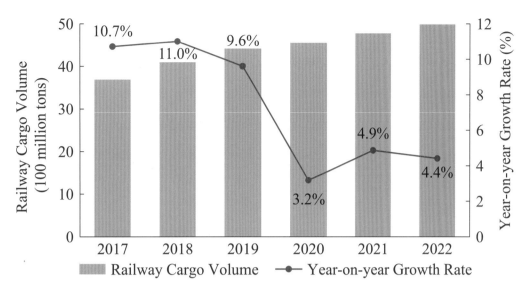

Figure 3-1: Changes in Railway Cargo Volume and Growth Rates from 2017 to 2022

In 2022, China's commercial highway cargo transport volume reached 37.12 billion tons, down 5.5% on a year-on-year basis. Turnover of cargo traffic reached 6.8958 trillion ton-kilometers, down 1.2% on a year-on-year basis. Cargo vehicle flow on expressways decreased by 10.4% on a year-on-year basis.

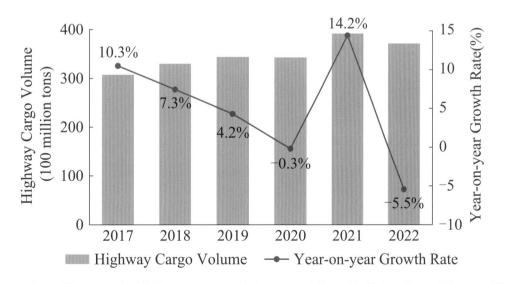

Figure 3-2: Changes in Highway Cargo Volume and Growth Rates from 2017 to 2022

In 2022, China's waterway cargo transport volume reached 8.55 billion tons, up 3.8% on a year-on-year basis. The number of inward and outward domestic trade cargo vessels decreased by 8.4% on a year-on-year basis. Turnover of cargo traffic reached 12.1003 trillion ton-kilometers, up 4.7% on a year-on-year basis.

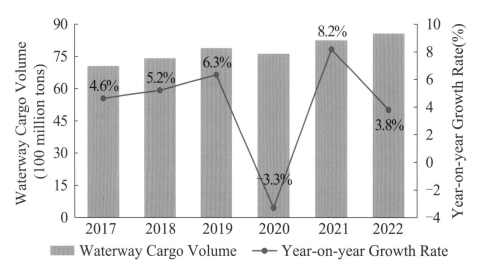

Figure 3-3: Changes in Waterway Cargo Volume and Growth Rates from 2017 to 2022

In 2022, China's port cargo throughput reached 15.68 billion tons, up 0.9% on a year-on-year basis, with a growth rate 5.9% lower than that in 2021. Specifically, the annual domestic trade cargo throughput and foreign trade cargo throughput reached 11.08 billion tons and 4.61 billion tons, up 2.1% and down 1.9% on a year-on-year basis, respectively. China's port container throughput reached 300 million TEUs, up 4.7% on a year-on-year basis, with a growth rate 2.3% lower than that in 2021. Domestic and foreign trade container throughput was 120 million TEUs and 170 million TEUs, up 3.6% and 5.4% on a year-on-year basis, respectively. Cargo throughout of port clusters around the Bohai Sea, the Yangtze River Delta, coastal regions of the Southeast China, the Pearl River Delta and coastal regions of the Southwest China was 4.46 billion tons of cargo,

2.65 billion tons, 710 million tons, 1.50 billion tons and 810 million tons, up 2.9%, 3.0%, 3.2%, down 3.8% and down 0.5%, respectively. Five major port clusters recorded total cargo throughput of 10.13 billion tons, accounting for 64.6% of the national port cargo throughput.

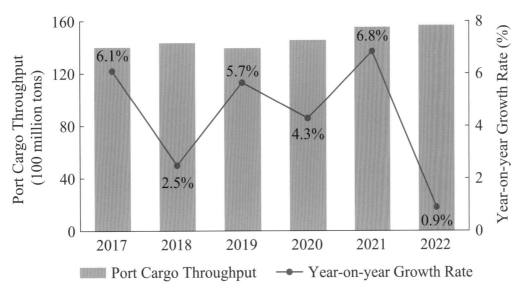

Figure 3-4: Changes in Port Cargo Throughput and Growth Rates from 2017 to 2022❶

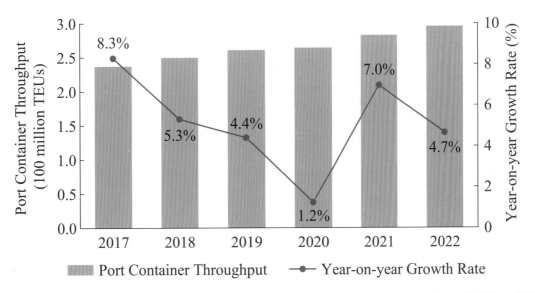

Figure 3-5: Changes in Port Container Throughput and Growth Rates from 2017 to 2022

---

❶ Since 2019, statistical caliber of ports has been adjusted to business entities with port operation licenses, and the growth rates have been calculated according to comparable caliber.

In 2022, China's civil aviation industry completed a cargo and mail transport volume of 6.08 million tons, down 17.0% on a year-on-year basis. Specifically, there were 3.44 million tons on domestic routes and 2.64 million tons on international routes, down 26.1% and 1.1% on a year-on-year basis, respectively. Turnover volume of cargo and mail traffic was 25.4 billion ton-kilometers, down 8.7% on a year-on-year basis.

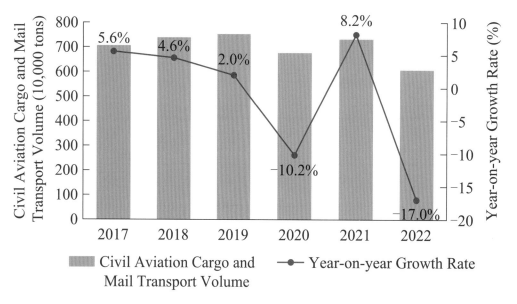

Figure 3-6: Changes in Civil Aviation Cargo and Mail Transport Volume and Growth Rates from 2017 to 2022

In 2022, China's postal industry completed 139.1 billion posting deliveries and 110.58 billion express deliveries, up 2.7% and 2.1% on a year-on-year basis, respectively. Specifically, there were 12.08 billion intra-city deliveries, 95.77 billion inter-city deliveries and 2.02 billion deliveries to other countries and regions including Hong Kong, Macao and Taiwan, down 9.3%, up 4.0% and down 4.1% on a year-on-year basis, respectively.

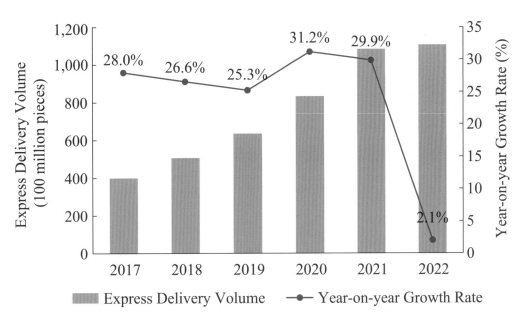

Figure 3-7: Changes in Express Delivery Volume and Growth Rates from 2017 to 2022

2. Constantly improved cargo organization efficiency: Railway cargo service efficiency was constantly improved. In the context of entirely upgraded 95306 Platform, the whole-process one-stop service of "one-off handling via one mobile phone on one website" was achieved. Centralized handling of cargo business was under full coverage. Per capita accepted cargo forwarding businesses and per capita waybills increased by 690% and 450%, respectively.

Road freight continued to transform and upgrade, and online freight developed in a standardized and efficient manner. 2,537 networked cargo enterprises pooled 5.943 million scattered transport vehicles and 5.224 million drivers in all sectors of the society, and completed 94.012 million waybills in the year. 31 cities in the third batch, such as Chengde, Langfang, Panjin, Tonghua, Lianyungang and Ningbo, participated in "Creation of Green Urban Cargo Transport Distribution Demonstration Project" and issued the *Administrative Measures for Green Urban Cargo Transport Distribution Demonstration Project.* Intensive, efficient, green and low-

35

carbon development of urban cargo transport distribution was accelerated. Brand publicity and promotion regarding rural logistics service continuously bore fruit.

The layout optimization was conducted for airline networks. Ports continued to take a fast track on digital transformation. Blockchain-based port electronic delivery of imported goods totaled 683,000 TEUs in 2022, up 138% on a year-on-year basis. The Beibu Gulf Port Qinzhou Automated Container Terminal was put into operation, which is the first of its kind in the world, with a U-shaped process layout to function with minimal manpower.

As the number of cargo aircrafts increased to 215 in China, their share in civil aviation transport fleet rose to 5.2%. Transport support continuously became more and more efficient. Application scopes of electronic waybill operation, green channel for special materials, electronic permit for cargo vehicles, and "single window" were further expanded.

General postal services were improved in both depth and breadth. Brilliant progress was made in project of "Express Delivery into Villages". Express delivery services were provided to 95% of administrative villages in China, while three or more deliveries were made to over 99% of administrative villages in western China every week. The collaborative development capacity of service industry was continuously enhanced. In 2022, there were 117 benchmark projects with over 10 million express delivery services for modern agriculture and 822 "One City, One Specialty" projects for postal services tailored to agricultural specialty. Satisfaction degree of express delivery service remained at a high level. Various indicators, such as the time limit of whole service process, 72-hour on-time delivery rate and valid complaint rate, turned better in all aspects.

Campaign of "Chain Strengthening and Chain Supplement of National Comprehensive Cargo Hubs" was launched, which supported the construction of comprehensive cargo hubs and collection, distribution and transport systems in 15 cities, and improved the efficiency and quality of comprehensive cargo transport, reduced comprehensive transport costs and shored up the stability of the industrial chain and supply chain. Multi-modal transport made faster progress. 46 multi-modal transport demonstration projects in the fourth batch were launched, and the demonstration lines were further added into main structure of the national integrated multi-dimensional transportation network and the national comprehensive transport hub cities. These demonstration projects registered an annual multi-modal container transport volume of about 7.2 million TEUs. China guided and propelled the construction of cargo collecting and distributing railway lines and promoted the business of "substituting container transportation for bulk and general cargo transportation" . Nationwide ports completed a railway-waterway multi-modal transport volume of 8.75 million TEUs in 2022, up 16% on a year-on-year basis. The *On Accelerating the High-quality Development of Cold Chain Logistics and Transport* were issued to promote the smooth, efficient, smart, convenient, safe and standardized development of cold chain logistics and transport.

(III) Continuously Improved Quality and Inclusiveness of Trip Services

1. Passenger transport continuously scaled down: In 2022, China's commercial passenger volume was 5.59 billion, down 32.7% on a year-on-year basis. Turnover of passenger traffic was 1.2922 trillion person-kilometers, down 34.6% on a year-on-year basis.

In 2022, China's railway passenger volume was 1.67 billion persons, down 35.9% on a year-on-year basis. The proportion of railway passenger volume of electric multiple units reached 76.2%, up 2.6% on a year-on-year basis. Turnover of passenger traffic was 657.8 billion person-kilometers, down 31.3% on a year-on-year basis.

In 2022, China's commercial highway passenger volume was 3.55 billion persons, down 30.3% on a year-on-year basis. Turnover of passenger traffic was 240.8 billion person-kilometers, down 33.7% on a year-on-year basis. As for passenger car transport, passenger cars with nine seats or less on expressways completed a passenger volume of 17.10 billion, down 21.4% on a year-on-year basis.

In 2022, China's commercial waterway passenger volume was 120 million, down 28.8% on a year-on-year basis. Turnover of passenger traffic was 2.26 billion person-kilometers, down 31.7% on a year-on-year basis.

In 2022, the civil aviation passenger volume was 252 million, down 42.9% on a year-on-year basis. Specifically, the number of passengers transported by domestic and international routes was 250 million and 1.86 million, down 43.1% and up 26.0% on a year-on-year basis, respectively.

Turnover of passenger traffic was 391.4 billion passenger-kilometers, down 40.1% on a year-on-year basis. Passenger load factor of regular flights was 66.6% on average in 2022, 5.8% lower than that in 2021.

In 2022, China's urban passenger volume was 75.51 billion, down 24.0% on a year-on-year basis. Specifically, the passenger volume of public buses and trams, urban rail transit, cruising taxis and urban passenger ferries reached 35.34 billion, 19.31 billion, 20.82 billion and 40 million, down 27.8%, 18.6%, 22.0% and 11.7% on a year-on-year basis, respectively.

2. Continuously improved quality of passenger transport services: Railway authorities precisely implemented train working diagram on a daily basis, flexibly allocated transport capacity according to demands, dynamically adjusted epidemic prevention and control measures at stations and trains, and continuously optimized passenger transport services. The *Catalogue of Prohibited and Restricted Items Carried and Consigned by Railway Passengers* and the *Administrative Measures for Real-name Registration System of Railway Passenger Tickets* were revised. Electronic payment for ticket extension was comprehensively implemented. New ticket system products were applied in 380 railway stations. Tourist-dedicated trains, such as "Western Tour Train" "New Oriental Express Train" and "Yunnan Tour Train", were put into service. Efforts were made to consolidate and outreach the effective synergy between poverty alleviation achievements and rural revitalization, and low-priced slow trains were still on track.

Conventional road passenger transport services were constantly transformed and upgraded, integrated development of new and old business patterns was accelerated, passenger transport services steadily progressed towards a state of convenient, useful and favorable for the people. The electronic-based passenger transport services were further refined. In China,

98.8% of passenger stations at grade-II and above conducted provincial-wide online ticket sales. Online tickets were sold via networking systems for the Ministry of Transport and provincial-level passenger stations in 22 provinces, and e-tickets accounted for more than 90% of the total volume. The *Guiding Operation for Scheduled Bus Passenger Transport Services* was formulated and implemented, and nearly 4,800 scheduled passenger transport lines were available all over the country. The *Guiding Opinions on Accelerating Integrated Development of Urban and Rural Road Passenger Transport and Tourism* was developed and introduced, with an aim to boost the integrated development of transport and tourism.

Integrated development of waterway passenger transport and tourism went further. Impetuses were given to the ongoing construction of 50 high-quality pilot waterway passenger transport routes. The Tourism Channel of the Tongzhou Urban Section of Beijing-Hangzhou Grand Canal was completed and started operation. Service quality of the Huangpu River Night Tour in Shanghai, the Yangtze River & Jialing River Night Tour in Chongqing and the Minjiang River Night Tour in Fujian was upgraded. The layout of cruise terminals was improved at a faster pace. *Guiding Opinions on Accelerating Development of Cruise and Yacht Equipment and Relevant Industries* was developed and introduced. Development and construction of Qingdao International Cruise Port Area made faster progress. Construction work of Zhanjiang International Cruise Port Complex Project formally commenced.

By the end of 2022, the number of domestic passenger airlines executed a total of 2.394 million flights, with an average flight regularity rate of 95.0% (7% higher than that in 2021). In the airports with an annual throughput of over 10 million passengers in the Chinese civil aviation industry, the rate of flight using jet bridge for boarding or disembarkation at terminal stands was 79.0%, up 2.1% on a year-on-year basis. The functions of civil aviation service quality supervision platform were continuously improved, and domestic airlines properly handled all complaints. 41 large airports with an annual throughput of over 10 million passengers provided "Easy Security Check" service. A total of 403,000 passengers were checked, and the average check duration was reduced by 38.7%.

By the end of 2022, urban rail transit was opened to traffic in 53 Chinese cities, including newcomers Nantong City and Huangshi City. Connectivity and convenience of urban rail transit were further enhanced. China continued to promote the priority development of urban public transportation and deepen the construction of a national public transportation city and issued the *Administrative Measures for National Transit Metropolis Construction Demonstration Project*. In 2022, dynamic assessment of 14 national transit metropolis construction demonstration cities (such as Beijing) and construction acceptance of 13 national transit metropolises (such as Chengdu) were completed, while 46 national transit metropolis construction demonstration cities were designated. New energy vehicles continued to be widely applied in the field of urban passenger transport, and the proportion of new energy buses was up to 77.2% in cities.

The construction of online ticketing systems for road passenger transport and ferry e-ticket systems in key waters accelerated. The application of e-tickets was increasingly popular. Research and development of key technologies and products for Mobility as a Service (MaaS) were under way in China Railway 12306 System. The scope of cooperation between the civil aviation passenger ticket system and China Railway 12306 System continuously expanded. Following China Eastern Airlines, Air China also cooperated with the railway authorities to seamlessly link the passenger ticket systems with selling air-rail passenger tickets. 12328 Transport Service Supervision Hotline System constantly improved functions and accepted 23.631 million cases in 2022, and its time-limited completion rate and callback satisfaction rate went up from 95.8% to 97.5% and from 98.9% to 99.7%, respectively.

Five practical actions in support of people's livelihood, including elderly-oriented design transport services, comprehensively bore fruit in 2022. More than 30,000 low-floor and low-entrance urban public buses and trams were added and updated, more than 2,700 urban bus lines were established to provide more convenience for the elderly, and more than 9,500 urban public bus and tram stops were renovated in an elderly-oriented manner throughout the year. The 95128 Car-hailing Service Hotline was put into service in more than 120 cities at the prefecture level and above, while nearly 300 cities launched "one-click car-hailing" , thereby facilitating more than 9.3 million elderly passengers. More than 4,000 subway stations across the country were equipped with accessible ramps. Accessible passage, parking spaces and toilet cubicles could be easily found in all expressway service areas in general.

Panel 3-1: Air-Rail Inter-modal Transport Product of Air China and China Railway

On December 27, 2022, the Cooperation Ceremony between Air China and China Railway & Air-Rail Inter-modal Transport Product Launch themed with "Integrated Development for Carefree Tour by Air and Rail" was jointly held by Air China and China Railway. Two sides announced the launch of a new air-rail intermodal product.

This air-rail inter-modal product can be used in a total of 30 cities, 50 transit railway stations and 282 non-stop railway stations, which covers Beijing, Shanghai, Guangzhou, Shenzhen, Chengdu and other key hub cities. Passengers can purchase high-speed rail and flight ticket package in Air China App and China Railway 12306 App. "One-off ticket purchase and payment for admission" greatly improves the whole process of passengers' ticket purchasing and trip experience.

(IV) Sound Development of New Transport Patterns

By the end of 2022, there were 298 licensed car-hailing platform companies, 5.09 million drivers and 2.118 million vehicles, up 15.5%, 28.9% and 35.9% on a year-on-year basis, respectively. Affected by the Covid-19 epidemic and other factors, 6.97 billion orders were completed in 2022, down 16.3% on a year-on-year basis. Online rental bicycles were put into operation in more than 460 cities. There were more than 15 million vehicles in operation and about 33 million orders were completed every day.

IV. Opening-Up and Cooperation

Chinese transport industry connected with the world and abreast with the times. In this context, the Global Sustainable Transport Innovation and Knowledge Center (GSTIKC) was established. China continued to deepen mutually beneficial cooperation with relevant countries in the field of transport, actively played its part in global transport governance, earnestly fulfilled its international responsibilities and obligations, and contributed to the vision of building a community with a shared future for mankind.

(I) Well-Established Transport Connectivity under the "Belt and Road" Initiative

Tongjiang-Nizhneleninskoye Railway Bridge (the first cross-river railway bridge between China and Russia), Heihe-Blagoveshchensk Road Bridge, China-aided Eastbay Expressway of Gwadar Port along China-Pakistan

Economic Corridor were opened to traffic. China-Laos Railway marked the first anniversary of its safe and stable operation. Lancang-Mekong Express freight trains achieved regular operation. Beno section of the Hungary-Serbia Railway was put into operation. The first test run of Jakarta-Bandung High-speed Railway met with a complete success in Indonesia. CHINA RAILWAY Express developed in a sound manner. By the end of 2022, 65,000 trains of CHINA RAILWAY Express delivered 6.04 million TEUs on 82 railway lines in service, connecting more than 200 cities across 25 European countries. A transport and logistics network basically took shape to embrace both Asia and Europe.

China saw continuously full-fledged international road transport agreement system, with the scope of cooperation expanded to 21 countries. It took only about two weeks for TIR-based road transport between Chinese inland cities and major European countries. Transport facilitation was steadily improved. International road transport routes, such as the route between China and Vietnam, were opened to traffic on a regular basis. International road transport corridors were further unimpeded.

China's waterway international transport routes covered more than 100 countries and regions, while maritime services benefited all coastal countries along the "Belt and Road". By the end of 2022, China had signed unilateral and bilateral agreements on the recognition of crew certificates with 27 countries along the "Belt and Road". Many ports with China as a stakeholder, such as Piraeus Port in Greece and Colombo Port in Sri Lanka, operated in good condition.

China has signed bilateral air transport agreements with 101 countries involved in the "Belt and Road" Initiative, and maintained regular passenger and cargo flights with 64 countries.

China Post rendered express services to more than 220 countries and regions.

Panel 4-1: China-Laos Railway: A Model for Regional Connectivity and Common Development

The first anniversary of the operation of China-Laos Railway fell on December 2, 2022. As a landmark project of high-quality co-construction of the "Belt and Road", China-Laos Railway transported a total of 8.5 million passengers and 11.2 million tons of goods in the first year of operation, including more than 1.9 million tons of cross-border goods. China-Laos Railway harvested brilliant fruits.

The 1,035-kilometer China-Laos Railway links Kunming, capital of Yunnan province, with Vientiane, capital of Laos.

Since the inauguration of China-Laos Railway, the railway authorities have innovated transport organization modes, such as "China-Laos Railway + CHINA RAILWAY Express" and "China-Laos Railway + China's New Western Land-Sea Corridor". Lancang-Mekong Express international freight trains have been put into service, enhancing the influence and cross-border freight capacity of China-Laos Railway.

China-Laos Railway improves the transport infrastructure conditions in Laos, raises the efficiency and professional level of local transport, greatly reverses the transport pattern in Laos, and effectively opens up the economic artery of Laos. China-Laos Railway is conducive to the connectivity between China and all countries on the Indo-China Peninsula, including Laos, thereby pushing forward the development of tourism and trade along this railway line, and jointly building a community of shared future featuring political mutual trust, economic integration and cultural inclusiveness.

(II) More Fruits of International Exchanges and Cooperation in Transport Realm

China constantly furthered policy dialogue in the field of transport with relevant organizations, countries and regions. China successfully hosted the First China-CELAC Transport Cooperation Forum, Maritime Day of China 2022 and the North Bund Forum. In the context of strengthened cross-border communication and coordination, China successfully convened important meetings, such as the First Meeting of the Working Group on Transport Cooperation of China-Laos Economic Corridor, the Third Meeting of the Working Group on Transport Cooperation of China-Myanmar Economic Corridor, the Ninth Meeting of the Working Group on Transport Infrastructure of China-Pakistan Economic Corridor and the 17th Round of Meetings of the China-Germany Cooperation Agreement on Inland and Waterway Transport, in an effort to further consolidate the consensus on cooperation. By working hard to diversify regional and sub-regional cooperation platforms, China exerted sustained efforts to advance and expand transport cooperation and exchanges with relevant countries and regions through regional cooperation mechanisms such as the Shanghai Cooperation Organisation, China-ASEAN (10+1) Cooperation Mechanism and China-CEEC Cooperation. Substantial progress was made in cooperation with the ASEAN in the fields of railway and road infrastructure construction, maritime transport, maritime affairs and air transport. Mutually beneficial and friendly transport cooperation was carried out by China and CELAC member states. China actively revised international conventions and technical regulations and submitted 114 proposals to the International Maritime Organization. China further played a leading role in the negotiations on greenhouse gas emission reduction by international shipping, propelled the formation of impartial and reasonable emission reduction solutions, and safeguarded the common interests of developing countries.

Panel 4-2: The First China-CELAC Transport Cooperation Forum was Successfully Hosted

On May 24, 2022, in order to implement the consensus as reached at the Third Ministerial Meeting of the Forum of China and the Community of Latin American and Caribbean States (China-CELAC Forum), the Ministry of Transport of the People's Republic of China, and the Ministry of Transport of Argentina holding the rotating presidency of CELAC, co-hosted the First China-CELAC Transport Cooperation Forum in the form of video conference. This Forum focused on the theme of "Enhancing Connectivity, Promoting Sustainable Transport and Contributing to China-CELAC Common Development".

Li Xiaopeng, Minister of Transport of China and Alexis Guerrera, Minister of Transport of Argentine attended and delivered keynote speeches. Ministers or representatives of transport authorities from other ten CELAC member states also attended and delivered speeches.

This Forum adopted the *Joint Ministerial Statement of the First China-CELAC Transport Cooperation Forum (2022)*, and announced the establishment of China-CELAC Transport Cooperation Forum, and expressed the prospects for future practical cooperation between the two sides in various forms in the professional fields of railway transport, road transport, waterway transport, civil aviation, logistics and maritime under the framework of this Forum. The second Forum will be held in 2025.

(III) Establishment of Global Sustainable Transport Innovation and Knowledge Center (GSTIKC)

On October 14, 2022, the Inauguration Ceremony of the Global Sustainable Transport Innovation and Knowledge Center (GSTIKC) was held in Beijing. Chinese President Xi Jinping sent a congratulatory letter to the establishment of GSTIKC, China's first working organization based on global sustainable transport development. GSTIKC is a permanent outcome of the Second United Nations Global Sustainable Transport Conference, which is of great significance to promote global transport cooperation and help build a community with a shared future for mankind.

Panel 4-3: Key Moves of GSTIKC

Promoting openness and connectivity: GSTIKC will organize various events including the Global Sustainable Transport Forum and establish a global cooperation network for sustainable transport development.

Promoting common development, equity and benefits for all: GSTIKC will develop into a knowledge-sharing platform and achievement demonstration platform in the field of global transport development.

Promoting innovation-driven development and activating growth drivers: GSTIKC will establish the Global Sustainable Transport Innovation Alliance, give impetuses to the development of smart transport and smart logistics all over the world, and push forward deep integration for new technologies (such as big data, the Internet, artificial intelligence and blockchain) to join hands with transport industry.

Promoting ecological prioritized, green and low-carbon transport: GSTIKC will carry out high-end people-to-people cultural exchange programs, dedicate to global capacity building for green and low-carbon transport, and facilitate more environmentally-friendly transport and low-carbon trip.

Promoting international cooperation and addressing global challenges: GSTIKC will build a top think tank for global sustainable transport development, implement global governance concept of "extensive consultation, joint contribution and shared benefits" , provide intellectual support for global sustainable transport development cooperation, and further enhance worldwide understanding and action capacity for sustainable transport.

V. Safety Emergency Response

Chinese transport industry put people and their lives first, actively pushed forward safe and high-quality industry development, strived to prevent and defuse major risks in the field of transport, constantly improved emergency support capabilities, and laid a solid foundation for sustainable transport development.

(I) Overall Stability of Transport Work Safety

General Secretary Xi Jinping's important instructions on work safety were thoroughly implemented. With focus on the goals and tasks set forth in the *Outline for the Construction of the Country with Great Transport Strength*, the *Outline of the National Integrated Transport Network Plan* and the *Planning for National Work Safety during the 14th Five-Year Plan Period*, a high-pressure and strict management stance was maintained, the work safety responsibilities were assigned to all parties concerned, the prevention and resolution of major risks were intensified, and persistent efforts were made to curb major accidents, reduce general accidents, and minimize the total number of accidents. The overall situation of work safety remained stable. In terms of railway transport, no particular serious or major traffic accidents occurred throughout the year, and death toll in railway traffic accidents decreased by 14.6% on a year-on-year basis. In terms of highway transport, no particular serious or major traffic accidents occurred throughout the year, with the number of serious accidents and death toll decreased by over 20% and 30% on a year-on-year basis, respectively. In terms of waterway transport, no particular serious accidents occurred throughout the year, with the number ❶ of accidents involving Chinese transport vessels and death toll (including number of missing persons) decreased by over 20% and 40% on a year-on-year basis, respectively. No major or serious accidents occurred in ports. In terms of civil aviation, the ten-year rolling value of major accidents per million flights was 0.011, and the accident rate per 10,000 flights for general aviation was 0.0367. The severe symptom rate per 10,000 hours for transport aviation decreased by 25.7% on a year-on-year basis, and the symptom rate per 10,000 hours attributable to human error decreased by 70.3% on a year-on-year basis. In terms of postal industry, no major work safety accidents and above occurred throughout the year, and casualty accidents at work sites decreased by 71.4% on a year-on-year basis.

---

❶ Transport vessel accidents include accidents causing deaths and accidents without deaths and missing persons.

(II) Further Intensified Supervision in Transport Safety

1. Transport safety management was continuously improved: Support for work safety system was reinforced, the quality and safety supervision of highway and waterway construction were enhanced, the standardization of transport work safety was continuously promoted, security plan for key information infrastructure on highways and waterways was issued, and safety assessments for principals and work safety managers of urban passenger transport companies were organized. Demonstrative centennial quality projects were under way in a proper manner. Greater efforts were made to address severe problems, while illegal passenger buses and overloaded freight trucks were investigated and penalized. 17,000 unqualified atmospheric-pressure dangerous liquid tankers fell into disuse, and the loading medium of 20,000 tankers was changed in 2022. By the end of 2022, the coverage rate of enterprises using electronic waybill for road transport of dangerous goods reached 85.3% in China, and the coverage rate of vehicles exceeded 66%.

2. Prevention and resolution of major risks in work safety went further: The preliminary "Whole Picture" of major risks in transport work safety was drawn, with a comprehensive inspection of over 2,800 major work safety risks. The three-year action for rectifying the safety environment along railway lines ended with brilliant outcomes. The safety facilities upgrading project covering 21,790 km and the disaster prevention and control project spanning 5,441 km were implemented for trunk highways. 13,774 old and dilapidated bridges on highways were renovated, and the safety and life protection project extending 135,000 km was carried out for rural highways.

The special three-year rectification for work safety and "100 Rectification Tasks" in transport were completed. In terms of civil aviation industry, special governance efforts including special investigations for engine faults as well as flight procedures optimization for small and medium-sized airports, especially complicated airports, were conducted. Safety control with risk grading and hidden danger resolution in urban rail transit operation were carried out profoundly.

3. Positive results were achieved in work safety: "Fifteen rigid measures" for work safety were put in place, the fulfillment of work safety responsibility was further strengthened, and severe and major accidents were effectively avoided. Documents such as the *Implementation Plan for Further Coordinating Development and Safety and Strengthening Transport Work Safety*, were formulated to vigorously ensure the safety and stability of major events including the Beijing Winter Olympics and Paralympics 2022 and important holidays.

(III) Continuous Improvement of Emergency Response Capacity

1. The building of emergency response capacity was continuously strengthened: Documents, such as the *Opinions of 23 Ministries and Organizations, Including the Ministry of Transport, on Further Strengthening the Capacity Building for Maritime Search and Rescue* and the *Guiding Opinions of the Ministry of Transport on Strengthening the Emergency*

Management System and Capacity Building for Transport were issued. The construction of National-level Regional Highway Traffic Emergency Equipment and Material Reserve Centers made steady progress. Pilot projects for maritime search and rescue emergency capacity building were launched, the second rescue flight team in the South China Sea was set up for direct hospital transfers of injured or ill personnel at sea, breaking the final barrier in "last mile" for maritime rescue. The construction of an oil spill emergency equipment depot was actively pushed. Stable progress was made in building salvage vessels, with 12,000-ton buoyancy-lifting salvage engineering vessels (5-6#) and 80,000-ton semi-submersible salvage engineering vessels being delivered and put into service. Projects of large-scale oil spill recovery vessel with corollary equipments were steadily advanced. Emergency response drill for comprehensive transport security under extreme weather during the Beijing Winter Olympic Games, the 2022 National Maritime Search and Rescue Comprehensive Exercise, the China-Laos-Myanmar-Thailand Lancang-Mekong River Joint Search and Rescue Desktop Exercise, China-United States, China-South Korea and China-Japan search and rescue communication drills were successfully held. BeiDou Navigation Satellite System joined Medium-altitude Earth Orbit Search and Rescue (MEOSAR). BeiDou Message Service System became part of the Global Maritime Distress and Safety System (GMDSS).

2. Emergency response was prompt and effective: Active response was made to sudden disasters, such as flash flood disaster in Datong County, Qinghai Province, the 6.8-magnitude earthquake in Luding County, Sichuan Province, etc. Accidents, such as the flight accident of China Eastern Airlines MU5735 on March 21, the derailment of bullet train D2809 on June 4, the windstorm disaster of crane ship "Fujing 001" on July 2, and the major road traffic accident in Sandu-Libo expressway, Qiannan Prefecture, Guizhou Province, were handled properly. Adequate preparations were made against typhoons such as Super Typhoon Hinnamnor and Super Typhoon Muifa, which fully ensure the safety of people's lives and properties. In 2022, maritime search and rescue centers at all levels took 1,588 rescue actions, dispatched ships for 12,225 missions and planes for 296 missions, successfully rescued 969 distressed ships and 9,748 distressed persons, with a success search and rescue rate of 96.4%.

Panel 5-1: National Water Rescue Forces

By the end of 2022, China had 24 rescue bases, three comprehensive salvage bases, six flight bases, more than 70 specialized rescue vessels, more than 140 salvage vessels, 20 rescue aerocrafts and 19 emergency rescue teams. At present, emergency rescue and support forces can be dispatched under the level-9 sea state and implement effective rescue under the level-6 sea state.

(IV) Stringent Epidemic Prevention and Control in a Scientific and Precise Manner

In accordance with the requirements of keeping the epidemic at bay, stabilizing the economy and ensuring safe development, efforts were made to implement policies, strategies and measures at all stages of epidemic prevention and control, adjust and optimize the prevention and control measures under specific circumstances in due time, conduct epidemic prevention and control of key aspects and high-risk positions, vigorously stop the spread of COVID-19 Pandemic, accurately and efficiently respond to COVID-19 clusters and sporadic outbreaks in some regions, implement the requirements for "managing COVID-19 with measures against Class B infectious diseases" , prevent and control the epidemic in transport industry in a scientific and precise manner, and let industry-wide epidemic prevention and control work take a steady and orderly turn.

VI. Scientific and Technological Innovation

China's transport sector upheld innovation-driven approach, enjoyed more growth drivers, and vigorously promoted the integration of new technologies (such as big data, the Internet and artificial intelligence) with the transport industry. Positive developments were achieved in scientific and technological outcomes and the construction of talent pool. Smart transport evolved by leaps and bounds with more scientific and technological innovation accomplishments were made.

(I) Greater Scientific and Technological Innovation Accomplishments

Reform of science and technology management went further, while research institutions turned increasingly mission-oriented and goal-oriented. Scientific and technological innovation quickened the pace in transport sector.

The *Outline of Medium and Long-term Development Plan for Scientific and Technological Innovation in the Field of Transport (2021－2035)* and the *Planning for Scientific and Technological Innovation in the Field of Transport during the 14th Five-Year Plan Period* were promulgated. Three scientific and technological projects, namely, key core technology breakthrough, traction application pilot of intelligent transport, and construction of scientific observation network for long-term transport infrastructure performance, were launched according to the *Planning for Scientific and Technological Innovation in the Field of Transport during the 14th Five-Year Plan Period*. Four industry-level key laboratories for integrated transport theory were recognized. 323 scientific and technological achievements were selected into Major Transport Scientific and Technological Innovation Results Library for Year 2022. Seven transport science and technology demonstration projects were initiated. Scientific research equipment support capacity was bolstered. By the end of 2022, key scientific and technological organizations in the field of highway and waterway transport possessed 332,000 units (sets) of scientific research equipment, an increase of 19,000 units (sets) compared with that in the late 2021, up 6.2%; 5,806 units (sets) of scientific research instruments and equipment worth RMB500,000 and above, an increase of 350 units (sets) compared with that in the late 2021, up 6.4%. Specifically, scientific research and technical service institutions, research institutions restructured into enterprises, colleges and universities and transport enterprises had 1,459 units (sets), 463 units (sets), 1,496 units (sets) and 2,347 units (sets), respectively. The *Action Plan for International Scientific and Technological Innovation in Transport under the "Belt and Road" Initiative* was formulated and implemented, further broadening the room for scientific and technological cooperation on a global scale.

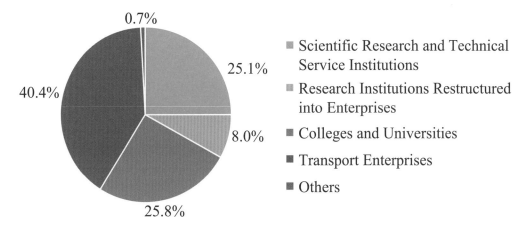

Figure 6-1: Proportions of Scientific Research Equipment
Worth RMB 500,000 and Above in 2022

(II) New Progress in the Development of Smart Transport

1. Robust progress was made in the construction of intelligent transport infrastructure: A number of new transport infrastructure application scenarios gradually came true. Key projects, such as Hangzhou-Shaoxing-Ningbo Smart Expressway, Nansha Port Area Phase IV Project in Guangzhou Port and Beijing-Hangzhou Canal Smart Waterway were launched at a faster pace. Special actions and pilots were carried out to digitize the infrastructure and safety emergency response of in-service trunk highways. Efforts were made to promote the construction of a bridge structure monitoring system for 644 highway bridge, as well as the summary and improvement of the national highway bridge infrastructure database covering 320,000 highway bridges across the country. A number of automated container terminals were built, including Taicang Port Area in Suzhou Port (Phase IV) and Berths No. 7-8 of South Operation Area, Dalanping Port Area in Qinzhou Port. By the end of 2022, a total of 14 automated terminals were built. The construction of a comprehensive digital waterway service platform for the Yangtze River trunk line was completed, which realized telemetry and telecontrol of more than 5,400 navigational beacons as well as telemetry and remote reporting of more than 160 hydrometric stations along the Yangtze River trunk line. Building Information Modeling (BIM) technology was increasingly applied in the Yangtze River waterway regulation and other projects.

2. Intelligent development of transport equipment accelerated: A new model of Fuxing High-Speed Comprehensive Inspection Train set a world record of 870 km/hour for open and in-tunnel track meeting speed of high-speed EMU trains. High Speed Flight Demonstration (HSFD) kicked off for C919, China's self-developed large passenger aircraft. Autonomous driving technology was constantly promoted and applied. Applications of auxiliary driving technologies, such as automatic emergency braking, lane departure warning, tire burst emergency response and tire pressure monitoring were carried out for road transport vehicles. China's first independently-developed oil-electric hybrid intelligent towing ship was put into use. "Jiangyuan Baihe", China's first 120-TEU pure electric inland river container ship, set off for maiden voyage. China's first 2,000-ton new energy transport ship "Dongxing 100", dedicated to collection and distribution, was put into operation.

3. Transport services constantly progressed towards intelligence: Sustained efforts were made to the construction of the industry information platform. The *Implementation Plan for National Comprehensive Transport*

Information Platform was issued. Efforts were made to aggregate and share the data. The concept of Mobility as a Service (MaaS) was publicized. Real-time information services for urban public transport were provided, while real-time forecast rate of incoming information on urban public trams and non-cash payment ratio constantly rose. The promotion of the electronic port and shipping operation documents and the construction of global blockchain-based shipping service network went further. In 2022, 815,000 TEUs of container cargo were electronically released, up 84.7% compared with that in the late 2021. Guidelines for the construction of blockchain-based electronic platform for dry bulk cargo import and export were formulated and implemented.

(III) New Achievement in Human Resources Development

Talent pool has been given focus as the primary resource and the construction of transport human resources was accelerated. Stress was laid on cultivating top-notch scientific and technological talents, developing talents through major engineering and technological innovation and research and development of key projects, relying on key laboratories and engineering research centers to gather talents, giving more supports for young scientific and technological talents, implementing the promotion plan for young scientific and technological talents in transport industry and other talents engaged in industrial scientific and technological innovation, and encouraging all types of industry-wide employers to establish and improve the support mechanism for leading talents and teams in scientific and technological innovation. Attention was paid to cultivating highly skilled personnel. New occupations were developed in transport, and professional standards were revised. National Finals of the 13th National Vocational Skills Competition of Transport Industry was held, which gave full play to steering role of vocational skills competition, underpinned the support for employees engaged in new transport patterns, offered favorable working environment, and rolled out a myriad of knowledgeable, skilled and innovation-oriented transport personnel. High-quality managers were intensively cultivated. Training was provided to improve their professional ability and quality, qualified personnel were selected and employed in a precise and scientific way, and outstanding young talents were vigorously cultivated and selected. The talent pool of transport sector was upgraded in quantity, quality, as well as its structure.

VII. Green Development

Chinese transport industry has unswervingly followed a path of prioritizing ecological conservation and pursuing green development, assumed the strategic task of sustainable transport development by promoting green and low-carbon transport transformation, boosted transport development towards carbon peaking and carbon neutrality objectives, and contributed to the vision of building a beautiful China.

(I) Elevated Overall Design of Green and Low-Carbon Transport Development

Overall design of green and low-carbon development was constantly improved in the field of transport. Steered by the goal of comprehensive green and low-carbon transport transformation, based on improvement of the transport equipment energy efficiency, efforts were made to optimize energy mix of transport, improve the efficiency of transport organization, and coordinate the green and low-carbon development of the transport industry. Green and low-carbon transport policy and standards became increasingly mature. Five environmental protection standards were issued to facilitate the formulation of the *Guidance for the Construction of National Carbon Peaking and Carbon Neutrality Standard System*. New progress was made in the green and low-carbon railway development, and comprehensive energy consumption per unit of transport volume kept at most 4.15 tons of standard coal per million converted ton-kilometers, a 1.2% down on a year-on-year basis. The *Action Plan for Green and Low-carbon Development of Highway Industry and Waterway Industry* was issued. In sustained Green Trip Initiative Action, 97 cities, including Beijing, reached the target, where green trips accounted for more than 70% and the satisfaction rate of green trip services exceeded 80%. Green Urban Freight Distribution Demonstration Project gained ground. Various activities were organized during Green Mobility Publicity Month and Public Mobility Publicity Week.

(II) Steadily Evolving Green and Low-Carbon Transport in Development Course

1. Transport structure was actively adjusted: *Work Plan for Optimization and Adjustment of Transport Structure for Development of Multi-modal Transport (2021−2025)*, which was issued by the General Office of the State Council, was put into practice. "Transit from highway to rail" and "transit from highway to waterway" in bulk cargo transport and medium-distance and long-distance cargo transport were accelerated. Efforts were made to improve the collection, distribution and transport system of port areas and parks. Special railway lines were vigorously paved in port areas, parks and factories. Multi-modal transport trunk channels were improved. Layout and construction of freight hubs were accelerated. Organization mode of multi-modal transport was innovated. Development of "through bill of lading system" and "whole-course single TEU system" was pushed forward in the field of multi-modal transport. Demonstration projects for multi-modal transport were further implemented. By the end of 2022, the national railway and waterway cargo turnover accounted for 15.9% and 53.5%, up 0.7% and 0.5% on a year-on-year basis, respectively.

2. Continued popularization of green and low-carbon transport facilities and devices: By the end of 2022, China's railway electrification rate reached 73.8%. China has built the world's largest and most widely distributed charging infrastructure network, with 5.2 million public and private charging infrastructures, up nearly 100% on a year-on-year basis. By the end of 2022, 17,581 charging piles were built in 4,145 highway service areas across the country. Specifically, 1,043 highway service areas were newly equipped with charging piles, and 4,207 new charging piles were added. The number of power stations increased to 1,973, up 52% compared with that in the late 2021. By the end of 2022, there were more than 540,000 new energy urban buses, nearly 300,000 new energy taxis, and more than 800,000 new energy urban delivery vehicles. The operation of ship LNG refueling stations was guided and supervised on the Yangtze River trunk line. Eight LNG refueling stations refueled 61 times with a total volume of 661.7 tons in 2022. Guangdong Province was supported to renovate more than 100 LNG-powered container ships. More than 5,200 shore power receiving facilities for ships were renovated in the Yangtze River Economic Belt. Ports and water service areas in 11 provinces consumed 74.97 million kWh of shore power, up 14% on a year-on-year basis. Significant progress was made in the use of shore power for ro-ro passenger ships in Bohai Bay, which used 5.05 million kWh of shore power, up 380% on a year-on-year basis. Technical regulations on hydrogen fuel cell-powered ships were promulgated in support of demonstration applications, such as electric ships and methanol-powered ships. Nationwide airports with annual passenger throughput of more than 5 million passengers installed and utilized alternate equipment of Auxiliary Power Unit (APU) to the utmost extent. "9917" Green Express Delivery Packaging Treatment Project was launched, namely, 90% of purchased and used packaging materials in line with the standards; 90% of standardized packaging operations, 10 million recycled express boxes, and 700 million recycled corrugated boxes by the end of 2022. Large-scale application pilot of recycled express packaging steadily gained ground.

3. Accelerated construction of transport carbon emission monitoring platform: In accordance with the goals of "one monitoring network, one set of authoritative data, one intelligent accounting and forecasting system and integrated management" , continued efforts were made to promote the construction of data governance center which brings together more than 70 types of data sources in terms of transport equipment and transport production. Construction of big data analysis centers constantly made progress. Deep mining and fusion analysis of multi-source and multi-dimensional data were initially achieved. Construction of decision support centers moved faster. Accurate calculation and prediction of energy consumption and carbon emissions under multiple transport modes, multiple energy types and multiple scenarios came true at a faster pace. Construction of a national ship energy consumption center was promoted. Technical requirements for ship energy efficiency were formulated, and the upgrading of shipping energy efficiency was propelled.

4. Further strengthened protection and restoration of ecological environment in transport industry: Green development mode of transport infrastructure, which obeyed the ecological conservation redline and suited to the carrying capacity of resources and the environment, went further. Coordinated and intensive use of railway and road resources, such as route positions and bridge sites, was promoted. Better performance was achieved in land saving and intensive use. Survey, design, construction and management of ordinary highways were further strengthened. The *Administrative Measures for Water Pollution Prevention and Control of Inland Waterway Vessels under 400 Gross Tons* were stringently enforced, thereby consolidating the good results of pollution prevention and control actions in ships and ports along the Yangtze River Economic Belt, improving the long-acting mechanism, and implementing regular dispatch notification system. Progress was made in construction of the monitoring and supervision experiment sites of ship air pollutant emission control in Shenzhen, Shanghai and Zhejiang.

VIII. Transport Governance

In 2022, reform of key transport segments continuously deepened in China. The construction of a unified and open transport market accelerated. Soft power of transport development was steadily enhanced.

(I) Continuous Improvements in Construction of the Institutional Systems

The *Railway Law of the People's Republic of China*, the *Regulations on Urban Public Transport*, the *Regulations on Rural Roads*, the *Civil Aviation Law of the People's Republic of China,* and the *Regulations on Investigation of Civil Aircraft Accidents* were amended in an orderly manner, accelerating the legislation of regulations urgently needed for the development of the industry. 42 departmental regulations were unveiled. The *Comprehensive Transport Standard System (2022)* was issued. The

Guidelines for the Construction of Intelligent Logistics Standard System, *Green Transport Standard System (2022)* and *Transport Safety Emergency Response Standard System (2022)* were issued, and 244 national and industry standards were published during the year. By the end of 2022, the transport industry possessed 3,925 standards, including 885 national standards and 3,040 industry standards. Seven international standards were officially released, including the *Railway Applications—Track Geometry Quality—Part 1: Characterization of Track Geometry and Track Geometry Quality* and *Portable Terminal Application with ITS Support Service—Part 2: General Requirements for Data Exchange Between Personal ITS Stations and Other ITS Stations*. China was elected as the chair of the Universal Postal Union (UPU) Geocoding Working Group to lead the compilation of the UPU geocoding international standard. Foreign versions of 31 standards, including *Technical Specification of Train Control Center*, *General Specifications for Design of Highway Bridges and Culverts* and *Unified Standard for the Application of Building Information Model in Port and Water Engineering*, were released.

(II) Deepening Reforms in Key Fields

The reform for coordinated administrative law enforcement was deepened, with the tasks, including institutional consolidation, integration of responsibilities and personnel transfer, accomplished. Efforts were made to advance the long-term mechanism for the standardization of law enforcement;

verify and rectify prominent issues in law enforcement on a regular basis; carry out a three-year initiative to enhance the quality and capacity of law enforcement personnel; and promote strict, standardized, fair and civilized law enforcement. Varied toll charging approaches were adopted, including charging by road sections, vehicle types, periods, entrances and exits, directions, and payment methods, which promoted differentiated charging of expressway tolls. By the end of 2022, 250 differentiated expressway toll charging policies were introduced in 29 provinces (no toll roads in Hainan and Tibet). In Hainan, pilot reform of mileage fee was carried out in an orderly manner. The taxi industry was further standardized, with improvements in institutional mechanisms for punishment of non-compliance, joint regulation, security of user funds, operational data management, and service quality and reputation assessment. The protection of rights and interests of those engaged in the industry was reinforced. 14 provinces issued corresponding work plans in response to the new forms of transport and standardized business operations. Efforts were made to continuously promote the protection against occupational injuries. Beijing, Shanghai, Chongqing, Sichuan, Jiangsu, Hainan, Guangdong and other provinces and municipalities carried out pilot work on the protection against occupational injuries for drivers registered with online car-hailing services. Positive results were achieved in the "Sunshine Action" for new-form platform enterprises in the transport industry. All major platform companies have announced the pricing rules and the upper limit of cut by news media, App and other means. Efforts were made to promote healthy development of the online car-hailing industry by publishing the situation of operation, data transmission, and compliance in major cities on a monthly basis, and having regulatory talks with major online car-hailing service providers, urging them to fulfill their responsibilities and operate in compliance with the law. The construction of "driver's home" was advanced, improving the resting environment for truck drivers. More than 1,300 "drivers' homes" were built and in service all over the country.

(III) Accelerated Construction of a Unified Open Transport Market

Efforts were made to advance the management of administrative licensing items, with implementation specifications formulated for 67 administrative licensing items and guidelines formulated for 38 ministerial-level items. Supervision of all fields and the whole chain before, during and after the event was promoted. The coverage and efficiency of trans-provincial operations were improved. A number of government services including inquiry and verification of the compliance certificate for shipping companies were added to the list of trans-provincial operation items. The application scope of electronic licenses for road transport was expanded, and 5.39 million electronic licenses were generated. More than 8.15 million general freight vehicles received the annual examination online. Mobile service replaced online service in the application for and approval of the permit for trans-provincial heavy-cargo transport. Port clearance efficiency was increased, and the port charges catalogue system was implemented. Four pilot reform measures targeting at the business environment for road transport, including information sharing in water-rail-air coordinated transport, were promoted nationwide. The implementation of services including extension of the hours for trucks to drive on city roads was advanced. The compliance information inquiry service for online car-hailing was optimized and offered to the public 8.1 million times. Efforts were made to implement the project of big data platform for public security in transport and accelerate the pilot application of "Internet + Regulation" targeting at illegal operations across provinces and illegal operation of vehicles engaged in the transport of hazardous goods. The application scenarios of credit supervision were expanded, innovative practices were carried out in terms of credit commitment, credit evaluation, punishment for dishonest behaviors, "Credit Ease Plus" and credit repair, and credit supervision by tiers and types was strengthened. Financial support policies for transport and logistics were issued, and the special refinancing policy for transport and logistics was extended till the end of June 2023. In 2022, the tax burden per unit of operating revenue fell by 15.4% in the transport industry.

(IV) Steady Progress in Transport Civilization

To tell transport stories well, focus was put on major thematic publicity activities, such as maintenance of smooth logistics, "Surging Rivers in China" and "Young Strivers" . Exhibition of "Forging ahead in the New Era" showcased development achievements of transport industry. To promote the spirit of the industry, publicity activities were carried out, including the "Annual Touching Figures of Transport" "Most Beautiful Port and Shipping Worker" "Most Beautiful Truck Driver" and "Most Beautiful Maritime

Worker". The torch bearers for the Winter Olympics and Paralympics and winners of the International Maritime Organization (IMO) Award for "Exceptional Bravery at Sea" in the transport industry were reported by the media. Continued efforts were made in the practice of "devotion, courtesy and honesty" and the publicity campaign of "civilized traffic and green mobility" as well as "My Bus, My City", with an aim to develop modern traffic civilization. Active efforts were made to develop science popularization bases and enrich national science popularization resources. 20 bases, including China Port Museum in Ningbo, Guangzhou Metro Museum, Shanghai Metro Museum and Museum of Civil Aviation University of China, were included in the second batch of national-level transport science popularization bases.

Epilogue

Development is the eternal theme of human society. Only with openness, inclusiveness and connectivity can countries reinforce each other's efforts and achieve win-win results. As the largest developing country, China always places its own development in the coordinate system of human development and creates new opportunities for world development through its own development. Chinese transport industry will consistently stay connected with the world and abreast with the times, promote the sustainable development of global transport, advance sustainable development of global transport, facilitate connectivity among countries, ensure the stability and smooth flow of global logistics supply chains, boost the development of world economy, and make due contributions to advancing the Global Development Initiative, putting the UN 2030 Agenda for Sustainable Development into practice, and building a community with a shared future for mankind.

Notes to the Report:

1. Statistical data of Hong Kong SAR, Macao SAR and Taiwan Province are not included in this Report. Some data are not the same in total and sub-total due to rounding.

2. "Operating vehicles on highways" within statistical scope refer to highway passenger and cargo vehicles registered in the highway transport authorities, which are in operation and have passed the latest annual review date in the past two years.

3. Commercial cargo transport volume refers to respective quantity completed by railway, highway, waterway or civil aviation, excluding pipeline data.

4. Commercial passenger volume refers to respective quantity completed by railway, highway, waterway or civil aviation, excluding the data of urban passenger transport. Specifically, commercial highway passenger volume only includes the traditional chartered bus passenger volume.

5. Highway passenger and cargo transport volume of 2022 includes the data of Xinjiang Production and Construction Corps. The national growth rate of highway passenger and cargo transport volume is calculated on a comparable basis.

6. Unattributed data in this Report are cited from the data of the Ministry of Transport of the People's Republic of China, the National Railway Administration of the People's Republic of China, the Civil Aviation Administration of China and the State Post Bureau of the People's Republic of China.